WHITE MAN, LISTEN!

013

Books by Richard Wright

Pagan Spain
The Color Curtain
Black Power
The Outsider
White Man, Listen!
Black Boy
12 Million Black Voices
Native Son
Uncle Tom's Children

WHITE MAN, LISTEN!

Richard Wright

With an Introduction by
Cedric Robinson

HarperPerennial
A Division of HarperCollinsPublishers

The Video Biography
Richard Wright—Black Boy
is available from
California Newsreel, 149 9th Street, San Francisco, CA 94103.
Telephone: 415-621-6196 fax: 415-621-6522

HarperCollins books may be purchased for educational, business, or sales promotional use. For information, please write: Special Markets Department, HarperCollins Publishers, Inc., 10 East 53rd Street, New York, NY 10022.

First HarperPerennial edition published 1995.

Designed by Caitlin Daniels

Library of Congress Cataloging-in-Publication Data

Wright, Richard, 1908–1960.
    White man, Listen! / Richard Wright. — 1st HarperPerennial ed.
       p.   cm.
    ISBN 0-06-092564-7
    1. Black race. I. Title.
   HT1581.W7   1995
   305.8'96073—dc20   94-44808

95 96 97 98 99 ❖/RRD 10 9 8 7 6 5 4 3 2 1

This book is dedicated to

My friend,
ERIC WILLIAMS,
Chief Minister of the Government of Trinidad and Tobago
and Leader of the People's National Movement;

and to

the Westernized and tragic elite
of Asia, Africa, and the West Indies—

the lonely outsiders who exist precariously
on the clifflike margins of many cultures—men who are
distrusted, misunderstood, maligned, criticized
by Left and Right, Christian and pagan—
men who carry on their frail but indefatigable shoulders
the best of two worlds—and who,
amidst confusion and stagnation,
seek desperately for a home for their hearts:
a home which, if found,
could be a home for the hearts of all men.

In every cry of every Man,
In every Infant's cry of fear,
In every voice, in every ban,
The mind-forg'd manacles I hear.

William Blake

Light breaks where no sun shines;
Where no sea runs, the waters of the heart
Push in their tides . . .

Light breaks on secret lots,
On tips of thoughts where thoughts smell in the rain;
When logics die,
The secret of the soil grows through the eye,
And blood jumps in the sun . . .

Dylan Thomas

Acknowledgments

For some of the many fragments of poems quoted in this volume I am indebted to the following authors:

Frank Horne, Langston Hughes, Robert E. Hayden, and Margaret Walker.

Particularly am I grateful to the editors of *The Negro Caravan*, Sterling Brown, Howard University; Arthur P. Davis, Virginia Union University; and Ulysses Lee, Lincoln University; for permission to quote from their most comprehensive anthology, *The Negro Caravan* (Dryden Press), fragments from the following authors' poems: Frances Ellen Harper's *Bury Me in a Free Land;* Albery A. Whitman's *Rape of Florida;* George Leonard Allen's *Pilate in Modern America;* Frank Horne's *Nigger;* Robert E. Hayden's *Gabriel;* Fenton Johnson's *Tired;* Claude McKay's *White Houses;* and Jean Toomer's *Song of the Son.*

I also wish to express appreciation to Harcourt, Brace and Company for permission to quote from W. E. B. DuBois's *A Litany at Atlanta;* to New Directions for permission to quote from Dylan Thomas's *Light Breaks Where No Sun Shines;* to Viking Press for permission to quote from James Weldon Johnson's *Saint Peter Relates an Incident;* to Random House for permission to quote James D. Corrothers' *At the Closed Gate of Justice;* and to Harper & Brothers for permission to quote from Countee Cullen's *Heritage.*

Also Viking Press was kind enough to allow me to quote generously from my own book, *12 Million Black Voices*.

To Arna Bontemps and to Melvin Tolson I am indebted for their personal permission to quote lines from *Nocturne at Bethesda* and *Dark Symphony* respectively.

And may I take this opportunity to express publicly my thanks to Dr. Otto Klineberg for his invaluable aid, guidance, and advice in helping me to devise a questionnaire with which I armed myself upon my first foray to grapple with the Asian personality? Needless to say, the interpretations which I drew from the results of that questionnaire are mine and are not to be laid at his door.

R. W.

Contents

Introduction to the HarperPerennial Edition by Cedric Robinson   *xiii*

Why and Wherefore, *Author's Introduction*   *xxvii*

1   The Psychological Reactions of Oppressed People   1

2   Tradition and Industrialization   45

3   The Literature of the Negro in the United States   71

4   The Miracle of Nationalism in the African Gold Coast   111

Introduction to the HarperPerennial Edition

Given the extremes of political and cultural repression imposed on America at the onset of the Cold War, one might surmise that the public, ritualized purging of Richard Wright by the State and the literati was merely a reflex, part of a general sweep of the incorrigibly dissident as well as the more manneredly critical. It was, after all, the beginning of an era for which Thucydides' summation of civil terror in *The Peloponnesian War* would be apt: "And they scrambled, in their judgments, the usual evaluations of actions as expressed by the words for them" (3.82.4). Wright, it might be presumed, was merely one—and only somewhat distinguishable by being Black—of the tens of thousands whose pasts provided material for a theater of intimidation. These essays will disabuse you of such notions. In them, Richard Wright provides evidence for the urgency of his selection by the political and cultural arbitrators who were neither casual nor indiscriminate. In the postwar years, Wright distinguished himself as a redoubt against the debasement of language and the politics it concealed. And in his resolve he employed his masterful eloquence as a writer and essayist to communicate a magisterial comprehension of the most powerful social, psychological, and cultural impulses implicated in the hegemonic politics of the West.

Written nearly four decades ago, these essays retain their analytical profundity, their capacity to shock by defamiliarization, and most significant, their authority to forge an original and independent construction of the historical and present forces that affect our lives. They confirm that Wright possessed a brilliant, troubled mind, a potent moral identity, and a singular reserve of courage. And courage was no small matter in this time of inquisitions. It was even more remarkable in one who, as a young boy in Mississippi, Tennessee, and Arkansas, had personally witnessed the beatings of black men and women and whose own family had experienced a lynching.

These essays, however, are not autobiographical; in them Wright rarely refers to his own experiences of the South ("I lived my childhood under a racial code, brutal and bloody . . ."). Rather than a regional focus or concentration on some particular cultural or political site of the world system, Wright's terrain is a civilization: the West and its potential destinies. Here his protagonists are drawn from the emerging elites of Africa, Asia, and the new world rather than the underclasses as in his earlier, more celebrated writings. And in two of the essays, "The Literature of the Negro in the United States" and "The Miracle of Nationalism in the African Gold Coast," he presents case studies of the genesis of these petite bourgeoisies into their epochal opposition to the West.

Wright's subject matter was not of his own choosing. Indeed, he appears to have sutured the concerns found in the writings of many of his contemporary Black radical intellectuals—Frantz Fanon, Aimé Cesaire, George Padmore, C. L. R. James, and Amilcar Cabral, to name the most illustrious. They, too, determined to trace the sociopsychological genesis of the historic appearance of a new social force: the revolutionary Black nationalist. What is extraordinary and distinctive in these essays is that in his interrogations Wright sought to illuminate the realities of a postcolonial world without the batteries of certainties, such as the scientist determinisms claimed by materialism (Liberal or Marxian), the inversion mazes of psychoanalysis, or what Wright maintains are the delusional deceits of religion.

Wright's political and intellectual odyssey began in the most desperate margins of the industrial world. Removed from slavery by the space of only one generation, Wright was born in 1908 on a sharecropper's plot near Natchez, Mississippi. Sharecropping and peonage, the lot of most Black rural workers in the early twentieth century, were systems of indebtedness that all but revived the human degradation of slavery. Accoutred with the official and informal mechanisms of racial terror, this labyrinth of poverty eventually took its toll on the Wright family. Abandoning the farm, Wright's father moved the family to Memphis, Tennessee, where he then deserted his wife and two sons. Wright's mother then sought refuge for her family with a married sister in West Helena, Arkansas. However, tragedy and violence had not yet exhausted themselves on this household: Wright's uncle, a saloonkeeper, was lynched; soon after, Wright's mother suffered a paralyzing stroke and Richard was placed in an orphanage. Wright and his mother returned to Mississippi to live with his maternal grandmother. In Jackson, Wright completed his formal education (the state considered the ninth grade sufficient for Blacks), and was recognized as his class valedictorian. A year earlier, as an eighth-grader, Wright had already distinguished himself: his short story "The Voodoo of Hell's Half-Acre" was published in three parts in Jackson's black newspaper, *Southern Register*.

Wright's immersion into the political economy of "negro labor" (clothing store porter, hotel porter, "errand boy") began at the age of sixteen. For a short while he worked in Jackson and then in late 1925 he moved back to Memphis. Already precocious and predelinquent, the teenaged Wright had gained entry into the most dangerous years of the young Black. In the cultural and political order of America, then and now, young Black males are imagined rapists and young Black females are presumed whores, and each is subjected to an appropriate discipline or abuse. As a Black menial laborer and resident in this delusional social order, Wright was confronted with its instrumentations: dehumanization, indifference, and patronage at the best of times, brutal intimidation, terror, and racial insults in the open season. In 1927, Wright migrated to Chicago, finding work as a porter. In 1929, he gained part-time entry into the post office (as a substitute clerk) and a doubly precarious place in blue-collar employment due to the worsening of the Depression.

As a seventeen-year-old in Memphis, Wright had continued his intellectual development informally. Barred by law from access to the public library, Wright secured novels and essays by using the borrower's card of a white friend. It was then that he determined to become a writer. In

Chicago, he discovered a very different sort of white patronage: the radical Left. Twenty years later, in the first of the essays here, Wright summoned up the significance of this encounter:

> Many an African in Paris and London, and many a Negro in New York and Chicago, crossed the class and racial line for the first time by accepting the ideology of Marxism, whether he really believed it or not. . . . [It] enabled the Negro or Asian or African to meet revolutionary fragments of the hostile race on a plane of equality.

One suspects this is Wright's postdoctrinal rendering rather than a more authentic account. Here, as in *American Hunger* (published posthumously in 1977) and its earlier version, "I Tried to Be a Communist" (1944), Wright required a phalanx of emotional and political shields, not the least of which was the contrition demanded of an ex-Marxist during the Cold War. Regardless, his ambivalence is apparent: in one moment he declares his skepticism of Marxism as a creed, and in another he validates the genuineness ("revolutionary fragments") of Marxists.

Wright's exposure to Marxist theory, radical doctrine, and the American Communist movement came during one of the most creative and active periods in the history of the American Left. During the Depression the Communist Party assumed the organizational leadership of progressive initiatives along a continuum of activity: Party members organized unions across racial lines among sharecroppers and poor farmers; orchestrated the defense of political dissidents and racial victims, such as the Scottsboro defendants; organized the unemployed; formed apprenticeship clubs for artists and writers; organized industrial workers; confronted pro-Fascist and other reactionary forces on the streets, in the political arena, and in popular culture; initiated petitions, fund-raisers, and community service organizations on behalf of the homeless and the hungry; and provided educational resources for the poor. The broader project of Marxism was of course the spawning of a revolutionary workers' movement, both a promise and, for Wright, "an interpretation of the world which impels to action."

The young man from Mississippi was fascinated by the activist "underground politics" of the Party, by the embrace of a political community infused with the liberation of the poor and the oppressed, and by the vision of a world revolutionary proletariat.[*] But he was distressed by other aspects of the movement: its theoretical absolutism and doctrinaire simplifications, the deceits concealed in Party discipline, the stultifying fealty to dogma demanded of intellectuals. Still the social delinquent, Wright was no better at submitting to Party authorities and dictum than to his earlier, racist domain. Indeed, he saw his work and presence as a necessary intervention to Marxist error: "The Communists, I felt, had oversimplified the experience of those whom they sought to lead."[†]

Nonetheless, Wright flourished within the Party's sphere, developing his craft as a journalist, essayist, and short story writer. He began work on *Cesspool,* a novel published posthumously as *Lawd Today;* he published poetry and short stories in such magazines as *New Masses, Left Front,* and *International Literature.* And while his reputation as a public lecturer and poet brought him increased recognition in left-wing circles, his wrenching short stories and powerful essays commanded their own audiences: "Big Boy Leaves Home" appeared in an anthology (*The New Caravan*) in 1936, and "Blueprint for Negro Writing" (*New Challenge*) in 1937. Indeed, by 1937, when Wright moved from Chicago to New York, he had become, in Daniel Aaron's estimation, "the Party's most illustrious proletarian author."[‡]

From the late 1930s, Wright was rushed into national and international celebrity. In 1938, the appearance of *Uncle Tom's Children* followed the receipt of a Guggenheim Fellowship. And then in 1940 *Native Son* was published, becoming the first work by a Black American to top the bestseller list (215,000 copies in the first three weeks, displacing Steinbeck's *The Grapes of Wrath*) and be selected for the Book-of-the-Month Club. Reconstructing its impact, Henry Louis Gates, Jr., suggests: "Never had the brute force of racism's crushing impact upon a

[*]Richard Crossman, *The God That Failed* (New York: Harper, 1965).

[†]*Ibid.,* p. 108.

[‡]Daniel Aaron, "Richard Wright and the Communist Party," *New Listener,* Winter 1971.

black consciousness been revealed before in fiction . . . reading often like a compelling detective novel or *policier noir* . . . the book performed a public, ritualized unveiling—the removal of the very mask of our blackness itself. Certainly the effect was like nothing before in the history of American letters."[*] Quite suddenly, Wright had become the foremost Black writer in American history with a literary and popular reputation far surpassing those of his predecessors. Within five years, Wright published *12 Million Black Voices* (1941) and *Black Boy* (1945), another bestseller; *Native Son* was adapted to the stage (directed by Orson Welles and starring Canada Lee); and in 1944, on the occasion of his public acknowledgment of his break with the Communist Party, he published "I Tried to Be a Communist."

Despite the phenomenal success of *Black Boy* and his elevation to international prominence, Wright became increasingly uncomfortable with America. In 1946, Wright, his wife, Ellen, and daughter Julia spent several months in France, a country that had become almost mythological among American Blacks for its reception of American expatriates and Black servicemen. For Wright this reputation was confirmed by the embrace of French intellectuals, the American colony, and the French public. Returning to New York, Wright was stung once again by the exclusion of Blacks from American culture and he resolved to protect his child from the onslaughts of racism. He relocated his family to France in 1947. Following his emigration, Wright would publish three major works, *The Outsider* (1953), *Savage Holiday* (1954), and *The Long Dream* (1958); a collection of short stories, *Eight Men* (1961); four nonfiction works, *Black Power* (1954), *The Color Curtain* (1956), *Pagan Spain* (1957), and *White Man, Listen!* (1957); and produced and starred in a screen adaptation (directed by Pierre Chenal) of *Native Son* (1951) filmed in Argentina. *Lawd Today* was published posthumously in 1963; *Island of Hallucination* remains unpublished.

Wright died at the age of fifty-two in Paris on November 28, 1960, survived by his wife, Ellen, and their daughters, Julia and Rachel. Though he had been ill for a year or more his death appeared sudden to

[*]Henry Louis Gates, Jr., and K. A. Appiah, *Richard Wright: Critical Perspectives Past and Present* (New York: Amistad, 1993).

many of his friends (Chester Himes, Ollie Harrington, Langston Hughes) and the circumstances suspicious. Clustered with the deaths of Black radical intellectuals George Padmore (1959) and Frantz Fanon (1961) under similar circumstances, coincidence was unpersuasive to some who knew him best. One of them, John A. Williams, would construct a *roman à clef, The Man Who Cried I Am* (1967), based on Wright's life during his expatriation in France, that attributed Wright's death to the Central Intelligence Agency. On the other hand, Michel Fabre, author of *The Unfinished Quest of Richard Wright* (1973) and Wright's most definitive biographer, remains skeptical. Unquestionably, during the twelve years of his European refuge Wright (and several of his Black American expatriate comrades) had been the constant subject of harassment and investigation by a multitude of powerful and mischievous official agencies: the CIA, the Federal Bureau of Investigation, the United States Information Agency, the State Department, British Intelligence, and, arguably, France's Sureté and Aliens Department. On this score he was not alone: many of the same agencies had targeted Black celebrities and intellectuals as politically dissimilar as Paul Robeson, W. E. B. Du Bois, William Patterson, Langston Hughes, Josephine Baker, Louis Armstrong, and Wright's fellow Black expatriates.[*]

Wright's political writings of his final decade constituted interventions: they were meant to achieve ruptures of the debauched moral cultures instituted and signified by the draconian state bureaucracies of the West and the East. The Cold War was orchestrated by a binary reductionism and, notwithstanding its public designation, frequented the poorer masses of Asia, Africa, Central America, and elsewhere with lethal, violent tours of neocolonialist and often covert maneuvers. Wright dismissed as fraudulent the claims of ethical superiority of the official contestants, the liberal democrats of the West and the Marxist-Leninists of the East. And his increased social and intellectual traffic with European dissidents and radicals, as well as with revolutionary nationalists from Asia and Africa, persuaded him that the hegemonic narratives of the era pinioned the actual champions of freedom and

[*]Mary L. Dudziak, "Josephine Baker, Racial Protest, and the Cold War," *Journal of American History,* September 1994.

democracy to an unreal contest. He thus pursued a critique of the postwar era that implicated an alternative historical agency, an alternative signification of liberation, an alternative reconstruction of modern history, an alternative epistemology of human desire. *White Man, Listen!* was the audacious product of that quest.

It would be presumptuous, of course, to attempt to determine for the reader the meaning as of these essays. Wright's own eloquence and his readers' own competencies would trivialize such an initiative. There are, however, political, historical, and literary demarcations pertinent to these essays that have been made fugitive by the passage of time, the intentional erasure of official and cultural authorities, or the social custom of deposing Black intellectuals to their "natural" terrain of race. Restoring some of these frames may prove useful.

These essays have their origins as lectures that Wright presented to university and public audiences in Italy, Germany, France, Sweden, Norway, and Denmark between the years 1950 and 1956. Their audiences are thus (silently) implicated in their analytical development as are the dramatic historical changes of this period and the energetic, restless mind of the author who sought to reconstitute the profound movements of modern society. His conceptual restlessness needs to be emphasized: in some moments Wright resorts to methodological individualism, his interest in existentialism coming to the fore or becoming more muted, providing license for explanations centered in psychoanalytic forces; at others, Wright weaves his way dialectically through the contest for priority between cultural and materialist approaches, nominating religion and reason as sometimes liberating and sometimes oppressive, valorizing and devalorizing technology and industrialism. He also exhibits a dissimilar commitment to style: Wright employs rhetorical models drawn from moral philosophy, the epic narrative, and the polemic.

At least for the immediate moment following the global paroxysm of World War II, Western imperialism was no longer defensible as either a moral or civilizing mission or even as the destined end of history. In the unmediated sites of colonialism in Asia, Africa, and the Caribbean, anticolonialist social and ideological forces manifested themselves into powerful nationalist movements; elsewhere, in what was to be designated the Third World, revolutionary, often Marxist, oppositions confronted the rule of the indigenous dominant classes. The social bases of anticolonialism consisted of disparate, often incongruous elements: ex-servicemen demobilized from the Allied armies; wage laborers who had been drawn to towns and cities by war production and transportation; rural laborers, peasants, and small-lot farmers; natives employed in the civilian infrastructure (nurses, civil servants, etc.); natives in small business and the professions, who expected greater advantages owing to their status; traditional authorities intent on restoring some of their precolonial autocratic protocols; technical and educated elites, trained in colonial colleges, universities, or military schools in the metropoles of Britain, France, Portugal, the United States, or the Soviet Union—the war had freed them all from the pernicious colonial social contract. And for rather complex reasons, the political leadership of the decolonizing impulses tended to be recruited from the educated elite.

Long before the war, colonial social orders had spawned anticolonial radicals like Padmore, James, Cesaire, Gandhi, Indira Gandhi, Nehru, Ho Chi Minh, Nkrumah, Azikiwe, Leopold Senghor, and the like. The war severely strained the British and French empires, mobilizing younger and sometimes more intense revolutionary nationalists. The postwar era became the setting of their initiatives: in India, China, Indochina, Iran, Madagascar, Algeria, Egypt, the Gold Coast, Nigeria, Kenya, South Africa, Puerto Rico, Guatemala, and elsewhere, national liberation movements took a militant and often rebellious form. Recruited to the leadership of these mass movements, the Westernized elites took full advantage of their intimacy with the West; many found, after long sojourns in the Western metropoles, that their nationalist objectives conflicted with their affection for bourgeois, industrial societies. And though Wright proudly claimed for himself a rootlessness, "a state of abandonment," it appears he acquired a sympathetic kinship with "those Asians and Africans who, having been partly Westernized, have a quarrel with the West." That quarrel formed the basis of "The Psychological Reactions of Oppressed People," an essay concerned with the immanent liberation emerging from the psychic and cultural ruins of colonialism.

Wright was a part of that West: he served his colonial peers as an intellectual beacon, as a symbol of their fugitive status in the West; in turn, as he moved among them at the Bandung Conference (1955), where the representatives of independent and aspiring Third World nations gathered, and jousted with them at the First Congress of Black Writers and Artists in Paris in 1957, Wright became more and more persuaded that the redemption of the modern world emanated from the Third World.

Wright's colonial contemporaries Fanon, Cesaire, Cabral, Padmore, and James undertook a similar pursuit. They, too, largely forsook orthodox Marxism in order to explore the uninterrogated domains of colonial life: the colonizers' employment of violence and the colonialist structuring of cultural systems of inferioritization; the Janus-like social and political identities of the native petite bourgeoisie; the moral degradation and cultural derationalization of the colonial metropoles; the revolutionary roles of the peasantry, of the lumpen proletariat, of impacted traditional cultures. Among the revolutionary theorists, it was Padmore who was most acutely disaffected with Marxism, announcing his embrace of Pan-Africanism. Wright, on the other hand, possessed a severe distrust of dogma. When John A. Williams wrote his introduction to the reissue of *White Man, Listen!* in 1964, he detected a hint of "dialectical materialism" in Wright's narratives, a Marxism that survived in Wright's consciousness by displacing the subject and agency of class with the subject and agency of color. Whether color or race could be substituted for class in any Marxian paradigm was of little concern for Williams, but it was precisely this issue with which Wright had wrestled for three decades.

Thus he ventured further, or perhaps differently, than the others: abandoning the cultural traditions that Cabral hoped to repair, dismissing the Marxism that Cabral and James sought to extend beyond its Eurocentric constrictions, and foregrounding a new nationalist elite, of which Cabral, Fanon, and James were suspicious. Isolated from his own native Black masses in America, Wright had none of the centering advantages and disadvantages of a Fanon embedded in the Algerian revolution, a Padmore deeply implicated in the Gold Coast's independence movement, a Cabral captaining the revolutionary movement in Guinea-Bissau, or even a James whose radical organizing extended from Britain, the United States, and the West Indies. Wright's base of operations was France, with its muddled Left intelligentsia. Thus it was the European

Left and its dialogue with its bourgeois counterparts which Wright addressed as his immediate audience.

Upon his embrace of armed struggle and revolutionary violence as a necessary psychocultural purgative for the "national bourgeoisie," Fanon had proclaimed: "If we wish to live up to our peoples' expectations, we must seek the response elsewhere than in Europe."[*] And though Wright had some sympathy with this Manichaean worldview, he felt it was risky to abandon completely European culture and Western international adventures to the Spartan whims of the technocrats germinated and nurtured by the contest between the superpowers. The Third World could only develop if the West and the Soviet worlds were held in check. As he informed his readers in the introduction to the French translation of *White Man, Listen!* (1959), it would be a catastrophe if Africans rehearsed "conflicts of the nature that plagued Europe and made her the bloody cockpit of the world for centuries, accounting for much of European mutual slaughter."[†] And though there he was addressing the schism between Catholic and Protestant, in the essays here, he made clear his inclusion of other ideological oppositions birthed in Europe.

Wright appropriated the task of interlocutor among Africa, the Third World, and the West. And because for the West the central actors in the historical drama were the Westernized elites, Wright was compelled to construct a sympathetic defense of this stratum. In these writings we can discover his tableaux of strategies, each designed to suture the odyssey of the Westernized elites to the intellectual domains familiar to the European mind: the existentialist didacticism of Heidegger, Kierkegaard, Husserl, and Sartre; the psychoanalysis of Freud and Octave Mannoni; the humanism of de Beauvoir, Sartre, and Arendt. And thus he audaciously implicated his Western audience in the conflicted fate of his fostered Third World kin through the intrigue of inhabited discourse. But perhaps even more important than these elegant, discursive structures, Wright employed the seductions of mutually recognizable oligarchies and the ensnaring persuasions of literary/rhetorical forms.

As he presented them, the Westernized elites were a new oligarchic

[*]Frantz Fannon, *The Wretched of the Earth* (New York: Grove, 1966), p. 255.
[†]Richard Wright, "To French Readers," *Mississippi Quarterly,* Fall 1989, p. 362.

element, poised in history to initiate and lead the reconstructions of their social orders, just as their postwar counterparts in the European intelligentsia were undertaking a parallel employment. As elites in a world contested by imperialism and anti-imperialism, by contending religious orthodoxies, by the extremes of poverty and wealth, and by secularism and tradition, it was their common task, their peculiar historical destinies, either to reinvigorate the economic, cultural, and political integrity of their nation-states or see them doomed to factionalism, strife, and possibly total erasure. Thus Wright insinuated his own existential angst into a currency of modern social identity.

Finally, as a student of Western literature, Wright employed rhetorical persuasion, drawing on the literary tropes deeply embedded in the cultural consciousness of Western intelligentsia. Part of the narrative authority of "The Miracle of Nationalism in the African Gold Coast"— beyond the dramatic power of the historic events themselves—emanates from its epic predecessor, Thucydides' *The Peloponnesian War.* Wright had visited the Gold Coast in 1953, interviewing some of the participants central to and on the margins of the independence movement, and published his impressions from that visit in *Black Power* (1954). In his essay, however, he chose the Thucydidean rhetorical device of imagining what his principals (Black Man Number One through Black Man Number Six) had debated in secrecy among themselves: "That must have been how much of the discussion went." Thus, just as C. L. R. James's treatment of the Haitian revolution (*The Black Jacobins,* 1938) and Du Bois's work on the Civil War and its aftermath (*Black Reconstruction in America,* 1935) had sought to situate the Black struggle in world history and literature, Wright used the device of cultural resonance to pose the African struggle as a heroic drama.

These essays, then, attest to Wright's mastery of literary form and cultural substance—they are the appropriate rejoinder to those who have maintained that Wright's creative imagination, command of his craft, and discernment as a social interpreter dissipated with his exile from America. These detractions were rooted not in his art or his thought but rather in the machine of criticism influenced by his political enemies and meeker souls. In contradistinction to the assault on his reputation, Wright's analytical skills and political wisdom continued to accumulate, and his courageous endeavors in the field of creative writing matched the expansion of his intellect, his historical consciousness, and his resolve to intervene in world events.

Wright understood the dangers involved in championing an alternative to the world order being fashioned by the two hegemonies, America and the Soviet Union. On a daily basis, he was forced into a pernicious intimacy with awesome political and cultural forces, even the mischievous machinations at their command. His resolve held. And though for a time the gatekeepers have been ascendant, particularly in the interval since his death, Wright's legacy has survived. Indeed, with the reissue of most of his writings, the publication of biographies, principled critiques, etc., we are now in the midst of a Wright revival. It can only be hoped that scholars and others among his present readers will exhibit a courage that matches that of Richard Wright.

—Cedric Robinson
The University of California
Santa Barbara

Why and Wherefore
Author's Introduction

    This book originated in a series of lectures delivered in Europe during the years 1950–56 in the cities mentioned below and under the following auspices: In Italy—in Turin, Genoa, and Rome—I lectured for the Italian Cultural Association; in Amsterdam, I addressed the Foundation for Cultural Co-operation (STICUSA, that is, *Stichting voor Culturele Samenwerking*); in Hamburg, I spoke under the joint auspices of the Congress for Cultural Freedom and the German publishing firm of Claassen Verlag; in Paris, I made two lectures for *Présence Africaine;* and, under the management of the great Swedish publishing house of Bonnier, I lectured in Stockholm, Uppsala, Oslo, Gothenburg, Lund, and Copenhagen. . . .

    None of these lectures was composed under the spur of personal motivation; they were written in response to repeated requests and, for the most part, with deep reluctance, for I do not particularly relish public speaking and always find myself unconsciously practicing a kind of malingering in preparing what I have to say until the very last moment.

    The idea of presenting these speeches in printed form never occurred to me until Bonnier suggested that they publish the four of them. It was then that I discovered that, by rearranging the order in which they were written, they made a comment, connected and coherent, upon white-colored, East-West relations in the world today.

The material dealt with in these addresses is admittedly explosive and blatantly unacademic, and the approach frankly subjective, though, as always, for the benefit of him who cares to read my lines attentively, I've scattered, with more than ample discursiveness, my value assumptions throughout the texts.

Upon rereading, I'm not inclined to want to alter anything in these discourses. With no attempt at special pleading or personal justification, I feel that responsibility, both political and social, informs every page, but that sense of responsibility has not made me curb my thoughts or censor my feelings. And I stand publicly behind every line I've written here.

When one is rash enough to commit oneself publicly upon issues as large and weighty as those contained in these lectures, one is naturally confronted with a cry for specifications, programs, platforms, and solutions; particularly is this comfort demanded with insistence by those who live uneasy lives in vast industrial civilizations where a hysterical optimism screens the seamier realities of life, hiding the quicksands of cataclysmic historical changes. In these pages, in which I've deliberately preserved the spoken tone, I'm much more the diagnostician than the scribbler of prescriptions. I'm no Moses and, as one great and shrewd American once said, if some Moses should lead you into the Promised Land, some other Moses, equally adroit and persuasive, could just as easily lead you out again.

To those who insist upon detailed and concrete plans of action, I can only urgently advise them to consult their congressman, their psychoanalyst, or, better still, if they are determined believers, their local priest. I can take this facetious method of answering with a good conscience because I'm convinced that we all, deep in our hearts, know exactly what to do, though most of us would rather die than do it.

I feel constrained, however, to ask the reader to consider and remember my background. I'm a rootless man, but I'm neither psychologically distraught nor in any wise particularly perturbed because of it. Personally, I do not hanker after, and seem not to need, as many emotional attachments, sustaining roots, or idealistic allegiances as most people. I declare unabashedly that I like and even cherish the state of abandonment, of aloneness; it does not bother me; indeed, to me it seems the natural, inevitable condition of man, and I welcome it. I can make myself at home almost anywhere on this earth and can, if I've a mind to and when I'm attracted to a landscape or a mood of life, easily sink myself into the most alien and widely differing environments. I must confess that this is no personal achievement of mine; this attitude was never striven for. . . . I've been shaped to this mental stance by the kind of experiences that I have fallen heir to. I say this neither in a tone of apology nor to persuade the reader in my ideological direction, but to give him a hinting clue as to why certain ideas and values appeal to me more than others, and why certain perspectives are stressed in these speeches.

Recently a young woman asked me: "But would your ideas make people happy?" And, before I was aware of what I was saying, I heard myself answering with a degree of frankness that I rarely, in deference to politeness, permit myself in personal conversation: "My dear, I do not deal in happiness; I deal in meaning."

Richard Wright
Paris

1

The Psychological Reactions of Oppressed People

Buttressed by their belief that their God had entrusted the earth into their keeping, drunk with power and possibility, waxing rich through trade in commodities, human and non-human, with awesome naval and merchant marines at their disposal, their countries filled with human debris anxious for any adventures, psychologically armed with new facts, white Western Christian civilization during the fourteenth, fifteenth, sixteenth, and seventeenth centuries, with a long, slow, and bloody explosion, hurled itself upon the sprawling masses of colored humanity in Asia and Africa.

I say to you white men of the West: Don't be too proud of how easily you conquered and plundered those Asians and Africans. You had unwitting allies in your campaigns; you had Fifth

Columns in the form of indigenous cultures to facilitate your military, missionary, and mercenary efforts. Your collaborators in those regions consisted of the mental habits of the people, habits for which they were in no way responsible, no more than you were responsible for yours. Those habits constituted corps of saboteurs, of spies, if you will, that worked in the interests of European aggression. You must realize that it was not your courage or racial superiority that made you win, nor was it the racial inferiority or cowardice of the Asians and Africans that made them lose. This is an important point that you must grasp, or your concern with this problem will be forever wide of the facts. How, then, did the West, numerically the minority, achieve, during the last four centuries, so many dazzling victories over the body of colored mankind? Frankly, it took you centuries to do a job that could have been done in fifty years! You had the motive, the fire power, the will, the religious spur, the superior organization, but you dallied. Why? You were not aware exactly of what you were doing. You didn't suspect your impersonal strength, or the impersonal weakness on the other side. You were as unconscious, at bottom, as were your victims about what was really taking place.

Your world of culture clashed with the culture-worlds of colored mankind, and the ensuing destruction of traditional beliefs among a billion and a half of black, brown, and yellow men has set off a tide of social, cultural, political, and economic revolution that grips the world today. That revolution is assuming many forms, absolutistic, communistic, fascistic, theocratistic etc.—all marked by unrest, violence, and an astounding emotional thrashing about as men seek new objects about which they can center their loyalties.

It is of the reactions, tortured and turbulent, of those Asians and Africans, in the New and Old World, that I wish to speak to you. Naturally I cannot speak for those Asians and Africans who are still locked in their mystical or ancestor-worshiping traditions. They are the voiceless ones, the silent ones. Indeed, I think that they are the doomed ones, men in a tragic trap. Any attempt on their part to wage a battle to protect their outmoded traditions and religions is a battle that is lost before it starts. And I say frankly that I suspect any white man who loves to dote upon those "naked nobles," who wants to leave them as they are, who finds them "primitive and pure," for such mystical hankering is, in my opinion, the last refuge of reactionary racists and psychological cripples tired of their own civilization. My remarks will, of necessity, be confined to those Asians and Africans who, having been partly Westernized, have a quarrel with the West. They are the ones who feel that they are oppressed. In a sense, this is a fight of the West with *itself*, a fight that the West blunderingly began, and the West does not to this day realize that it is the sole responsible agent, the sole instigator. For the West to disclaim responsibility for what it so clearly did is to make every white man alive on earth today a criminal. In history as in law, men must be held strictly responsible for the consequences of their historic actions, whether they intended those consequences or not. For the West to accept its responsibility is to create the means by which white men can liberate themselves from their fears, panic, and terror while they confront the world's colored majority of men who are also striving for liberation from the irrational ties which the West prompted them to disown—ties of which the West has partially robbed them.

Let's imagine a mammoth flying saucer from Mars landing, say, in a peasant Swiss village and debouching swarms of fierce-looking men whose skins are blue and whose red eyes flash lightning bolts that deal instant death. The inhabitants are all the more terrified because the arrival of these men had been predicted. The religious myths of the Western world—the Second Coming of Christ, the Last Judgment, etc., have conditioned Europeans for just such an improbable event. Hence, those Swiss natives will feel that resistance is useless for a while. As long as the blue strangers are casually kind, they are obeyed and served. They become the Fathers of the people. Is this a fragment of paperback science fiction? No. It's more prosaic than that. The image I've sketched above is the manner, by and large, in which white

Europe overran Asia and Africa. (Remember the Cortés-Montezuma drama!)

But why did Europe do this? Did it only want gold, power, women, raw materials? It was more complicated than that.

The fifteenth-, sixteenth-, and seventeenth-century neurotic European, sick of his thwarted instincts, restless, filled with self-disgust, was looking for not only spices and gold and slaves when he set out; he was looking for an Arcadia, a Land's End, a Shangri-la, a world peopled by shadow men, a world that would permit free play for his repressed instincts. Stripped of tradition, these misfits, adventurers, indentured servants, convicts and free-booters were the most advanced individualists of their time. Rendered socially superfluous by the stifling weight of the Church and nobility, buttressed by the influence of the ideas of Hume and Descartes, they had been brutally molded toward atti-tudes of emotional independence and could doff the cloying ties of custom, tradition, and family. The Asian-African native, anchored in family-dependence systems of life, could not imagine why or how these men had left their homelands, could not con-ceive of the cold, arid emotions sustaining them. . . . Emotional independence was a state of mind not only utterly inconceivable, but an attitude toward life downright evil to the Asian-African native—something to be avoided at all costs. Bound by a charged array of humble objects that made up an emotionally satisfying and exciting world, they, trapped by their limited mental horizon, could not help thinking that the white men invading their lands had been driven forcibly from their homes!

Living in a waking dream, generations of emotionally impover-ished colonial European whites wallowed in the quick gratifica-tion of greed, reveled in the cheap superiority of racial domina-tion, slaked their sensual thirst in illicit sexuality, draining off the dammed-up libido that European morality had condemned, amassing through trade a vast reservoir of economic fat, thereby establishing vast accumulations of capital which spurred the industrialization of the West. Asia and Africa thus became a neu-rotic habit that Europeans could forgo only at the cost of a powerful psychic wound, for this emotionally crippled Europe had, through the centuries, grown used to leaning upon this black crutch.

But what of the impact of those white faces upon the personalities of the native? Steeped in dependence systems of family life and anchored in ancestor-worshiping religions, the native was prone to identify those powerful white faces falling athwart his existence with the potency of his dead father who had sustained him in the past. Temporarily accepting the invasion, he transferred his loyalties to those white faces, but, because of the psychological, racial, and economic luxury which those faces derived from their domination, the native was kept at bay.

Today, as the tide of white domination of the land mass of Asia and Africa recedes, there lies exposed to view a procession of shattered cultures, disintegrated societies, and a writhing sweep of more aggressive, irrational religion than the world has known for centuries. And, as scientific research, partially freed from the blight of colonial control, advances, we are witnessing the rise of a new genre of academic literature dealing with colonial and post-colonial facts from a wider angle of vision than ever possible before. The personality distortions of hundreds of millions of black, brown, and yellow people that are being revealed by this literature are confounding and will necessitate drastic alteration of our past evaluations of colonial rule. In this new literature one enters a universe of menacing shadows where disparate images coalesce—white turning into black, the dead coming to life, the top becoming the bottom—until you think you are seeing Biblical beasts with seven heads and ten horns rising out of the sea. Imperialism turns out to have been much more morally foul a piece of business than even Marx and Lenin imagined!

An agony was induced into the native heart, rotting and pulverizing it as it tried to live under a white domination with which it could not identify in any real sense, a white domination that mocked it. The more Westernized that native heart became, the more anti-Western it had to be, for that heart was now weighing itself in terms of white Western values that made it feel degraded.

Vainly attempting to embrace the world of white faces that rejected it, it recoiled and sought refuge in the ruins of moldering tradition. But it was too late; it was trapped; it found haven in neither. This is the psychological stance of the elite of the populations, free or still in a state of subjection, of present-day Asia and Africa; this is the profound revolution that the white man cast into the world; this is the revolution (a large part of which has been successfully captured by the Communists) that the white man confronts today with fear and paralysis.

"Frog Perspectives"

I've now reached that point where I can begin a direct descent into the psychological reactions of the people across whose lives the white shadow of the West has fallen. Let me commence by presenting to you concept number one: "Frog Perspectives."

This is a phrase I've borrowed from Nietzsche to describe someone looking from below upward, a sense of someone who feels himself lower than others. The concept of distance involved here is not physical; it is psychological. It involves a situation in which, for moral or social reasons, a person or a group feels that there is another person or group above it. Yet, physically, they all live on the same general material plane. A certain degree of hate combined with love (ambivalence) is always involved in this looking from below upward and the object against which the subject is measuring himself undergoes constant change. He loves the object because he would like to resemble it; he hates the object because his chances of resembling it are remote, slight.

Proof of this psychological reality can be readily found in the expressions of oppressed people. If you ask an American Negro to describe his situation, he will almost always tell you:

"We are rising."

Against what or whom is he measuring his "rising"? It is beyond doubt his hostile white neighbor.

At Bandung, Carlos Romulo of the Philippines said:

"I think that over the generations the deepest source of our own confidence in ourselves had to come from the deeply rooted knowledge that the white man was *wrong,* that in proclaiming the superiority of his race, *qua race,* he stamped himself with his own weakness and confirmed all the rest of us in our dogged conviction that we could and would reassert ourselves as men. . . ."

The "we" that Romulo speaks of here are the so-called "colored" peoples of the world. It is quite clear here that it is against the dominance of the white man that Romulo measures the concept of manhood. Implied in his statement is the feeling or belief that the white man has, by his presence or acts, robbed the colored peoples of a feeling of self-respect, of manhood. Once more we are confronted with the problem of distance, a psychological distance, a feeling that one must regain something lost.

At Bandung, in 1955, President Sukarno of Indonesia spoke as follows:

"The peoples of Asia and Africa wield little physical power. Even their economic strength is dispersed and slight. We cannot indulge in power politics. Diplomacy for us is not a matter of the big stick. Our statesmen, by and large, are not backed up with serried ranks of jet bombers."

Listen to the above words with a "third ear" and you will catch echoes of psychological distance; every sentence implies a measuring of well-being, of power, of manners, of attitudes, of differences between Asia and Africa and the white West. . . . The core of reality today for hundreds of millions resides in how unlike the West they are and how much and quickly they must resemble the West.

This "frog perspective" prevails not only among Asians and Africans who live under colonial conditions, but among American Negroes as well. Hence, the physical nearness or remoteness of the American or European white has little or nothing to do with the feeling of distance that is engendered. We are here dealing with values evoked by social systems or colonial regimes which make men feel that they are dominated by powers stronger than they are.

"The 'Whiteness' of the White World"

This "frog perspective" which causes Asians, Africans, American or West Indian Negroes to feel their situation in terms of an "above" and a "below" reveals another facet of the white world, that is, its "whiteness" as seen and felt by those who are looking from below upwards.

It would take an effort of imagination on the part of whites to appreciate what I term "the reality of whiteness" as it is reflected in the colored mind. From the inside of an American Black Belt, from the perspective of an African colony where 90 per cent of the population is black, or from China, India, or Indonesia where the white man is a rare sight or a distinct minority, the Western white world shrinks in size. The many national states which make up that white world, when seen from the interior of colored life lying psychologically far below it, assumes a oneness of racial identity. This aspect of "whiteness" has been reenforced by a "gentleman's agreement" (of centuries' standing) implemented by treaties and other forms of aid between the big colony-owning powers to support one another in their colonial difficulties. Of course, of late, there have been some exceptions to this rule. For example, today Germans are prone to boast that they and they alone among the European powers have no record of recent exploitation of Asians and Africans. The Americans can say that they were largely responsible for the liberation of Indonesia. And when the Germans and Americans say this they are expecting that Asians and Africans make a distinction between them and the other colony-owning European states. Yet this distinction is hardly ever made. Why? Because the "whiteness" of Europe is an old reality, stemming from some five hundred years of European history. It has become a tradition, a psychological reality in the minds of Asians and Africans.

I have on occasion heard an Englishman express horror at the French policy in North Africa; and I've heard Frenchmen condemn both the British and the American systems of racial practices. On the other hand, the Spanish claim that they and they alone treated the colored peoples fairly and justly: they married them, etc. In making these boastful claims of their virtues in dealing with their colored colonial subjects, all of these European nations forget that they are contending with a reality which they themselves created deep in the minds of their subject people.

Whose hands ran the business enterprises? White hands. Whose hands meted out the law? White hands. Whose hands regulated the money? White hands. Whose hands erected the churches? White hands. Thus, when the white world is viewed from inside the colored world, that world is a block-world with little or no divisions.

I've heard liberal-minded Frenchmen express genuine horror at the lynching of a Negro by Mississippi whites. But to an Asian or an African it was not a Mississippi white man who did the lynching; it was just a Western white man. It is difficult for white Western Europe to realize how tiny Europe is in the minds of most of the people of the earth. Europe is indeed one world, small, compact, white, apart. . . .

"THE NON-WESTERN SENSE OF 'TIME'"

In Asia and Africa white Westerners are always expressing astonishment at the fact that they are referred to by the native elite as "aggressors." Indeed, Westerners find that this accusative tone of the Asian-African elite is not limited to those living under colonial rule, but, strangely, also embraces those Asians and Africans who have already gained their freedom. The surprise of the West at this resentment reveals a singular poverty of imagination, for it indicates a failure on the part of the West to appreciate the magnitude, the intensity, and the depth of distortion which its impact has wrought upon the lives of its accusers.

The average European white lives far from the realities of colonial rule and, therefore, gives little or no thought to the plight of the Belgium Congo natives or the millions of blacks whose earthly destinies are dictated by Frenchmen; such repellent facts, if they are known at all, are casually rationalized under the well-intentioned but mystically enigmatic rubric: "Well, when they are as evolved as we are, they'll be free too." While the continued subjugation of millions of Africans constitutes a *fait accompli* for the bulk of Western whites, there exist legions of liberal-minded Westerners who would register genuine moral horror at what transpires in those geographical prisons known as colonies, if they ever saw one. Thus, intellectual isolation and moral laziness conspire to render the mentality of the Westerner stoutly resistant to the revolution launched by his own kind in the emotional life of the Asian-African elite, a revolution that has shaped its content and guided its orientation.

For example, practically the whole of the non-Westerner's conception of historic "time" is charged with a sense of hot urgency deriving from the fact that his feel of that "time" almost invariably refers to, just as it most certainly stems from, the date of the European occupation of his country. In their marathon and frantic discussions of their dilemma, the most habitual verbal reference on the lips of the non-Western elite is: "*After the coming of the white man . . . ,*" or, "*Before the coming of the white man . . .*" In the Asian-African mind there is a gaping historic "time" displacement whose vital dimensions and dynamism are unguessed at by whites who reckon their historic sense of "time" in more general and relaxed terms of such remote, non-racial, and "superhuman" events as the birth of Christ, etc. But the Asian or African, trapped in the net of European trade and religion and yet suspended in his own daily tribal rituals, cannot escape the profound, contrasting cleavages wrought in his world by Western pressure. Hence he feels that the historic "time" that has the most decisive meaning for him dates from his "awakening" consequent to white Western intervention in his existence.

"WHO AND WHAT IS A 'SAVAGE'?"

Most Asians and Africans know that the word "savage" is frankly derogatory and is meant, when it is used, to demean them and create moral sanction in the public mind of the West for the continued dominance, political and/or economic, of Europe over them and their people. But, in my questioning of the Asian-African elite, I have found that the word "savage" had a far different, a psychologically double-edged, connotation and was not at all as simple as white Westerners would have it. In fact, Asian-African definitions of the word "savage" shed more light upon the mentality of the Europeans who used it than the objective reality that that word was supposed to describe.

An intuitive African scholar analyzed the word "savage" in the following terms:

"There *is* such a phenomenon as a 'savage,' but it's not what the Europeans think it is. Europeans are much too intimately involved in the creation of the 'savage' to be able to describe him objectively.

"You'll find our tribal life quiet, regimented; our villages are orderly, clean, our people obedient to tribal authority. If there's anything wrong in our tribal life, it's its deadly boredom broken only by religious ceremonies. . . . But, when Europeans yank a tribal man out of his tribe, shattering his orientation to his world, and inject him suddenly into a new and completely different sphere of living with other assumptions, that tribal man becomes emotionally confused, finds himself acting upon a wide range of conflicting values. His actions become erratic; he tries too quickly to fuse disparate elements into an impossible whole under the condescending monitoring of nervous Western tutors whom he seeks to please and, at the same time, struggles to keep peace in his own torn heart.

"Such behavior, when viewed by uncomprehending and unsympathetic outsiders, seems bizarre, contradictory, and it's undoubtedly from this artificially induced and warped behavior that the word 'savage' takes its meaning, for 'savages' are the products of a Western, a morally imperialistic, influence upon us, a wrong kind of an attempt to 'change' us. But the white missionary, who is largely responsible for the erratic behavior that goes by the name of 'savage,' can never understand that that which he calls our 'savage' behavior is the consequence of his zeal to 'save.' . . . Convinced that he is appointed by God for his mission, he is psychologically bound, in defense of his self-esteem, to brand any tribal man a 'savage' who fails to heed his call to salvation or to adjust to his standards, never suspecting that he is thereby unconsciously ridding himself of moral blame for his inept proselytizing."

"THE RESENTMENT OF 'EVOLUTION'"

Perhaps no word in the lexicon of the West is rejected more vehemently by the African living under French rule than the word "*evolué*" as it is applied to his gradual transition from the state of "savagery" to the level of "civilization." Above all, he resents bitterly the biological implications of the word, a reaction that few or no Europeans suspect. The word "*evolué*" means in French: to perform evolutions, to turn, etc. Perhaps the American-British socioanthropological definition, *acculturation* (the approximation of one social group or people to another in culture or arts by contact) or its equivalent (maybe the word "absorption" would be better!) would evoke less offensive reactions. Or is the word "*evolué*" used, as many cynical French-African students contend, expressly to provoke psychological hesitancy, self-doubt—the necessary emotional reactions that would intimidate the black neophyte and create in him the feeling that he can never really make the "civilized" grade? The sheer vagueness of the word would seem to suggest this. And who is to determine when the African candidate has sufficiently "*evolué*" toward an acceptable level of "civilization"? Only when he rises *en masse* and, putting knives at the throats of his rulers, chases them out? To date that seems to have been the only *de facto* criterion.

"THE PROJECTION OF 'ROMANCE'"

One sizzling April afternoon, in 1955, I sat in the pressroom of the Bandung Conference listening to a hard-bitten young Indonesian national revolutionary as he related some of his hair-raising exploits at sea against the Dutch. As he talked a young white newspaperwoman entered on the far side of the room. At once my informant broke off his narrative, leaned forward, and pointed.

"You see that woman?" he asked me.

"Yes," I said.

"I was talking to her last night in a hotel bar," he said, settling back in his chair and laughing nervously. "Boy, is *she* in love with the island of Java! She raves about the red clay, the statuesque beauty of our naked peasants, the wild orchids, the soft breezes in the morning, the extinct volcanoes, the high and fluffy clouds, and the incredible blueness of our skies. . . . She says that our dances make her drunk with ecstasy. She swears that romance and poetry steep every moment of our lives, and that we oughtn't ever change our way of living in order to be like the West." He paused and stared. "There must be something lacking in the lives they live in the West that make them act like that." Suddenly he straightened in his chair and pulled aside the lapel of his Palm Beach coat and allowed the dun-colored tip of a hand grenade to peep forth. "Boy, if she'd known that I had one of these little babies nestling in each armpit, she would've fainted. . . . Ha ha ha . . . ! What do those people think we are?"

"The Suspicion of 'Stupidity'"

"They want us to be stupid and they want to keep us stupid" is a statement I have heard scores of times both in Asia and Africa. What the Asian or African means by this is that he feels that the white West does not want him to develop to the same heights, or in the same way and manner, that the West has developed. Now, I cannot say if such an attitude is actually a reality in the minds of Western whites. I can only report that this suspicion that the white man wishes that the Asian and African remain in their tribal or "primitive" state is most certainly a reality in the Asian and African mind. When whites hold this outlook, the Asian and African feel that they detect an attitude of racial jealousy on the part of the white man.

"The moment that we become industrialized, they can no longer treat us as they did in the past" is another widespread statement among the elite of Asia and Africa. Put plainly, the Asian or African is prone to feel that the West strives to hinder the development of Asians and Africans who would compete with the white West on a plane of equality, or even some day attain a position of superiority. In short, the Asian and African feel that the race for industrialization is, in part, a "racial" race, that is, a "racial" competition. It is obvious that the concept of industrialization here has been wrenched by force of psychological reaction out of its normal historical context and harnessed to the dubious service of "racial" pride. In this direction it would be well to remember that the reality of an industrialized Russia figures symbolically and beckoningly large. Quailing before the tragic cost of Russia's industrialization, the elite of Asia and Africa frantically seeks for short cuts to avoid such wholesale expenditures of human life in order to become self-reliant and secure. Stalin's World War II motto of: "The side with the most motors will win" has sunk home in their hearts, but they can find as yet no humane method of arming themselves with the necessary motors.

This "suspicion of stupidity" causes the Asians and Africans to examine the most objective and liberal advice of white Westerners with care, probing for the "hidden jokers," searching for the "trap," the "gimmick," the "angle," that would keep the white West in a position of perpetual historical dominance. And many Western whites, who naively and unthinkingly accept their present status of dominance as natural, unwittingly feed the distrust and suspicion in Asian and African minds by superior attitudes borrowed from past historical contexts. Thus, longing ardently for conditions of industrialization, the Asian and African have come to feel that any display of industrial might and finesse on the part of the white West is for the purpose of intimidating them, of making them feel inferior. Missionaries who enter the continents of Asia and Africa with gleaming cars are resented; advertisements of television sets, washing machines, etc., are viewed with the necessary protective scorn; qualitative assessments of Western figures of production are sneered at at the very moment when the elite of Asia and Africa is desperately seeking ways and means of duplicating such figures in its own homelands.

Deceit? Hypocrisy? No. As this analysis of psychological reactions unfolds, you will see that such traits are thrown up by factors more powerful than the individuals involved, and it would be well to remember that I am here dealing with psychological "reactions" and not psychological "actions."

"WHAT IS A 'WHITE MAN'?"

The "white man" is a distinct image in Asian-African minds. This image has nothing to do with biology, for, from a biological point of view, what a "white man" is is not interesting. Scientifically speaking the leaders of Asia and Africa know that there is no such thing as race. It is, therefore, only from a historical or sociological point of view that the image of "white man" means anything. In Asian-African eyes, a "white man" is a man with blue eyes, a white skin, and blond hair, and that "white man" wishes fervently that his eyes remain forever blue, his skin forever white, and his hair forever blond, and he wishes this for his children and his children's children. Today I'm sure that the billion and a half colored people of Asia and Africa would be more than willing to sign a most solemn covenant guaranteeing that the Western "white man's" eyes shall remain forever blue, his skin forever white, and his hair forever blond. White Europe need not fear today regarding the purity of its blood stream. But what the Asian and African will not agree to is that the oil, the diamonds, the bauxite, the timber, the copra, the tin, the manganese, and the gold of this earth belong to the "white man" merely because his eyes are blue.

Any educated African, Asian, or American Negro who would seek to deny or negate the "whiteness" of white Europe would be branded by his colored brothers as being "white struck," as being "too Western," as having gone "white man." (The above phrases that I've used have occurred in correspondence which I've

received from Africans, Asians, and American Negroes within the
last few months.) Indeed, any man of color who seeks to give
even an objective account of how "colored people" feel will often
be accused of "mulatto thinking." Because I have sometimes questioned the modern serviceability of African culture, many
Africans have criticized my thinking as "white thinking." Any
Egyptian today who would marry a European would be considered disloyal by his compatriots.

This "whiteness" of the white world, this "frog perspective,"
this pathos of distance that I've been describing—these are not
static qualities; they have their dynamic aspects which I shall now
proceed to present to you.

"NEGATIVE LOYALTY"

The foremost quality of action which one finds among so many
colonial peoples is a kind of negative loyalty to the West among
the educated elite. This negative loyalty is a kind of yearning under
almost impossible conditions to identify with the values of the
white world, since their own traditions have been shattered by that
world. Perhaps this yearning to identify with the values of the
white world is stronger among American Negroes and West Indian
Negroes than any other sections of the colored people in the
world. The reason for this is simple: The Negroes in America and
in the British West Indies live within the confines of the white cultures that dominate them—cultures that limit and condition their
impulses and actions.

Let me illustrate this from the American Negro point of view.
The Negro American is the only American in America who says:
"I want to be an American." More or less all the other Americans
are born Americans and take their Americanism for granted.
Hence, the American Negro's effort to be an American is a self-
conscious thing. America is something outside of him and he
wishes to become part of that America. But, since color easily
marks him off from being an ordinary American, and since he
lives amidst social conditions pregnant with racism, he becomes

an American who is not accepted as an American, hence a kind of negative American.

The psychological situation resulting from this stance is a peculiar one. The Negro in America is so constantly striving to become an American that he has no time to become or try to become anything else. When he becomes a publisher, he is a "Negro" publisher; when he becomes a physician, he is a "Negro" physician; when he becomes an athlete, he is a "Negro" athlete. This is the answer to the question that so many people have asked about American Negroes: Why do not American Negroes rebel? Aside from the fact that they are a minority and their rebellion would be futile, they haven't got time to rebel. Why are Negroes so loyal to America? They are passionately loyal because they are not psychologically free enough to be traitors. They are trapped in and by their loyalties. But that loyalty has kept them in a negative position.

This negative loyalty is widespread also in Asia and Africa. The elite that I've met in Asia and Africa were striving desperately to build societies most nearly like those of the Western states. Nkrumah, Nasser, Sukarno, Nehru, are all Western-educated men striving to make a Western dream come true in non-Western conditions of life. They too share with the American Negro certain negative aspects of loyalty. Each of the four men I've named has come under heavy criticism by white Westerners. (This tragic problem of the elite I shall deal with a little later.)

The psychological dynamics of the Westernized non-Westerner, that is Western-trained and educated Asians and Africans, assume truly strange and compounded psychological patterns. The stance of negative loyalty leads to a whole variety of ironic attitudes. I shall describe this reality briefly under the heading of *acting*.

"ACTING"

What? Am I saying that Asians and Africans and colored people in general are good actors? No. I'm not speaking of the theater. I'm saying that the situation of their lives evokes in them an almost unconscious tendency to hide their deepest reactions from those who they fear would penalize them if they suspected what they really felt. Do I mean to imply that Asians and Africans and American Negroes are not honest people, that they are agents of duplicity? I do not. They are about as honest as anybody else, but they are cautious, wise, and do not wish to bring undue harm upon themselves. Hence, they act. Let me recite an experience of mine. I recently had lunch one day, in Paris, with an Englishman interested in Asia and Africa, and with a West Indian Negro social scientist. The Englishman kept asking me questions about Asians', Africans', and American Negroes' reactions to their plight, and I kept answering quite openly and frankly. I noticed, as I talked, that the West Indian Negro social scientist kept glowering at me, shaking his head, showing acute evidence of something akin to anger. Finally he could contain himself no longer and he blurted out:

"Wright, why are you revealing all of our secrets?"

Unwittingly, I had hurt that man. Desperately I sought to allay his feelings. I had thought that we were three free, modern men who could talk openly. But, no. The West Indian Negro social scientist felt that I was revealing racial secrets to the white race.

"Listen," I said, "the only secret in Asia and Africa and among oppressed people as a whole is that there is no secret."

That did it. He threw up his hands in disgust and exclaimed:

"You have now revealed the profoundest secret of all!"

The scope and intensity of this Asian-African and Negro acting depend on the degree of white hostility that they confront. In America, this acting is a perfected system; it is almost impossible for the white man to determine just what a Negro is really feeling, unless that white man, like a Gunnar Myrdal, is gifted with a superb imagination. In a recent interview William Faulkner, Nobel Prize winner, declared that he could not imagine himself a Negro for two minutes! A strange statement to come from a man with an undoubtedly rich imagination. The American Negro's adversary is next door to him, on the street, on the job, in the school; hence, acting has become almost a second nature with him. This acting regulates the manner, the tone of voice, even, in which most American Negroes speak to white men. The Negro's voice is almost always pitched high when addressed to a white man; all hint of aggressiveness is purged from it. In some instances an educated Negro will try to act as uneducated as possible in order not to merit rebuff from whites.

In Asia and Africa this acting exists, but in a looser form. Not being as intimately related to the Western white man in their daily lives as the American Negro, the Asian and African do not need to practice this dissimulation to the degree that the American Negro does. Yet it is there. There are Asians and Africans who, when confronting whites, will swear proudly that they have never felt any racial feelings at all, that such feelings are beneath them, and will proceed to act in a Western manner. Yet, when alone or among themselves, they will confess their feelings freely and bitterly. I believe that it was only at Bandung that the full content of Asian and African racial feelings were expressed publicly and for the first time in all their turgid passion. They were among themselves and could confess without shame.

This "acting" is one of the secrets that my West Indian social scientist did not want me to talk about. He felt that I was making the Negro, the Asian, and the African transparent, vulnerable to white attack. On the other hand, it is my conviction that the sooner all of these so-called secrets are out in the open, the sooner both sides, white and colored, realize the shadows that hem them in, the quicker sane and rational plans can be made. Let us go one step further into this business of secrets.

The educated Asian, African, or American Negro who longs to escape his debased position, who longs to have done with acting, who longs to convert his negative loyalty into something positive, will encounter ideology sponsored by labor leaders or revolutionaries, the most powerful and appealing of which is that of Marxism. In short, one minority section of the white society in or under which he lives will offer the educated elite of Asia and Africa or black America an interpretation of the world which impels to action, thereby assuaging his feelings of inferiority.

Nine times out of ten it can be easily pointed out that the ideology offered has no relation to the plight of the educated black, brown, or yellow elite. Yet, what other road is there out of his Black Belt? His captured homeland? His racial prison? But that ideology does solve something. It lowers the social and racial barriers and allows the trapped elite of Asia and Africa and black America the opportunity to climb out of its ghetto. In Asia almost all the national revolutionaries I met had received aid from the hands of Marxists in their youth. The same was true of the black politicians of the Gold Coast, even though Marxism did not even remotely pertain to their non-industrial society. The same is true of the Negro in the United States where there prevailed an absurd theory, Marxist in origin, that the Negro constituted a separate nation.

"IDEOLOGY AS INTIMACY"

The fear inspired by white domination breeds a tendency, as I have said, to make Asians and Africans act, pretend. And this same almost unconscious tendency to pretension will spur them to pretend to accept an ideology in which they do not believe. They accept it in order to climb out of their prisons. Many a black boy in America has seized upon the rungs of the Red ladder to climb out of his Black Belt. And well he may, if there are no other ways out of it. Hence, ideology here becomes a means towards social intimacy.

Yes, I know that such a notion is somewhat shocking. But it is true. And in your heart, you know it's true. Many an African in Paris and London, and many a Negro in New York and Chicago, crossed the class and racial line for the first time by accepting the ideology of Marxism, whether he really believed it or not. The role of ideology here served as a function; it enabled the Negro or Asian or African to meet revolutionary fragments of the hostile race on a plane of equality. No doubt the oppressed, educated young man said to himself: "I don't believe in this stuff, but it works." In the Gold Coast young revolutionary Africans told me that, as soon as they had gained their freedom, they were going to erect a statue to the English white woman, thereby celebrating friendships that had redeemed days and weeks of loneliness. "If it had not been for them, we would have lost," they told me.

"RESISTANCE"

Now, the most natural reaction, the most human response, to the revelation I've just made is to reject it and declare that no such psychological reaction exists. And the tendency to deny psychological traits of the sort I've just revealed leads me to my next concept: Resistance. There is a state of mind among the elite of Asia and Africa and the Negroes of America to reject that which they imagine hurts, degrades, or shames them. It is painful to realize that one is not free enough to make clean and honest decisions, that one has to "use" ideologies for one's own personal benefit. It is a state of mind that compels people to protect themselves against truths that wound; it is a deep, unconscious mechanism that prompts one to evade, deny, or seek explanations for problems other than those that prevail, for one does not wish to acknowledge a state of affairs that induces a loss of face.

I had the experience in both Asia and Africa of receiving intimate, unprompted confessions of how Indonesians felt about the Dutch, of how the Africans felt about the British, but as soon as those confessions appeared in print, there were hasty and passionate denials on the part of the very men who had given me their confessions.

Oppressed people have two sets of feelings: one for home consumption and one for export. I must say in all fairness that this duality of attitude has really aided the Asian and African in his dealing with white Westerners. In almost every instance of colonial revolt, the white Westerner has had absolutely no inkling of the revolt until it burst over his head, so carefully hidden had the rebels kept their feelings and attitudes. In short, oppression helps to forge in the oppressed the very qualities that eventually bring about the downfall of the oppressor.

"Flight Into the Past"

Not all evasion or resistance on the part of the subject people is so positive. Much of it is a flight into useless identification. One hears much in America about "Negro genius"; one hears much in Africa about vanished "glories of past empires"; in Asia one hears much of "our wonderful traditions that go back a thousand years." All of this, of course, is an attempt to prove that, though smarting under a sense of inferiority, they are the equals of those who oppress them. If the present is painful, then seek shelter in the warm womb of the past.

Let us push on into this uncharted area of human reactions and discover even more fantastic mental landscapes. Let us recall the "frog perspective"; let us recall the tendency to "act"; let us remember the will to resist the acknowledgment of facts that cause pain, and the tendency to retire to the haven of past "glories." In the light of all this, is it surprising that one discovers that religion among oppressed peoples is no longer a way of determining one's relation to the world, but has turned into a way of asserting pride? How can one's religion turn into pride?

The white West entered the vast continents of Asia, Africa, and even the Americas in the name of religion. (Of course, they took a lot of gold and silver and slaves while preaching religion, but it was in the name of religion that their actions were rationalized.) After five hundred years of white Western domination in the name of a superior religion, I found the ancient religions among the masses in those areas more or less intact. How is that possible? There was no doubt but that the missionaries had labored hard. There was no doubt but that the Asians and Africans had been converted by the hundreds of thousands to the Christian church. How was it then, that after five hundred years, the delegates at Bandung passed a resolution to resurrect their old religions and cultures and modernize them? Obviously, those religions were never really dead.

At the world conference of black writers, artists, and intellectuals in Paris, in September 1956, the main and only resolution called for the rehabilitation of their ancient cultures and religions! And, more significant, at that conference African Christians launched an attack upon Christianity, calling for its de-Europeanization. In other words, the religious tie between Africa and Europe was under vigorous attack not by Communists, but by African Christians themselves. Why?

Well, let your minds go back a little. Remember the burden of the message carried by the Christian missionaries into Asia and Africa? The Asian and African felt that the Christianity in whose name he had been conquered was really his own religion slightly disguised! Here is how he looked at it. Christianity came from one and perhaps unrepeatable historical accident that was compounded in Rome from Greek science and love of human personality, from Jewish notions of a One and Indivisible God, from Roman conceptions of law and order and property, and from a perhaps-never-to-be unraveled amalgamation of Eastern and African religions with their endless gods who were perpetually sacrificed and their endless virgins who gave birth perennially.

(May I add here, quite frankly, that, in part, I agree that some of the work of the missionary was good: I agree that his boiling down four hundred gods and six hundred devils into *one* God and *one* Devil was an advance. But I don't think that the missionaries' efforts went far enough; they should have reduced the whole problem to a psychological project.)

When Christianity met the so-called pagan religions of Asia and Africa, there was a strange result. How could Asia and Africa reject a militant Christian religion, at least, upon its initial impact? There was too much in that Christian religion that the Asian and African had believed in long before the Christian religion ever came to their shores, for it had been from the shores of Asia and Africa that these powerful legends, myths, images, symbols, and rituals had originally come. But the return of Christianity to the place of its birth was no peaceful homecoming; it came with fire in its eyes, a sword in its hands, and with the will to conquer and despoil. Why, then, did the elite in Asia and Africa accept it? When I put this question to an African scholar in the Gold Coast three years ago, I got the following answer:

"We've got four hundred gods. Jesus Christ. God number 401."

What happened was quite simple. When the white Westerner, armed and powerful, received a submissive attitude from the Asian and African, he took it for granted that the Asian or African had accepted his religion. The Asian and African had pretended to accept it to stave off attack, to receive petty favors. But the building of railroads, factories, and mines in the colonies, and the introduction of wage-rate labor, and the general spread of secular ideas, ate slowly away at the native religions, not destroying them completely, but rendering them truncated.

Despite the fact that his old, ancestral religions were made useless, made a mockery, the Asian and African never really abandoned them. He kept his religion to show that he was still a human being. Religion became a matter of human pride. The white man said: "I have the only one and true religion." The Asian and African replied, silently to be sure, but nonetheless passionately, "We have a religion too." *

"INDUSTRIALIZATION BECOMES RELIGION"

But, in time, a new religion replaced the truncated one. The Asian and African saw that techniques and industrialization had enabled the white man to enter his land and, in hoping for freedom, he found that the only road out was to embrace techniques and industrialization. Indeed, industrialization soon became the new religion, not because industrialization itself was loved or revered as a means of production, but because it was the only way to hoist the white man off his back.

Do you not see how facts change their aspects, their meaning, under the pressure of oppression? So strong and widespread is this

---

*Under the religiously toned spur of a new Indian nationalism, the reverse process is under way in India today. Thousands of Hindu Christians are being de-Christianized in popular and public ceremonies.

tendency for facts to be seen by the oppressed from a special point of view that I've called this a Metamorphosis of Facts. Religion turns into pride. Industrialization turns into religion. Race consciousness emerges as shame and bitter defiance. And in many instances sexuality assumes the means by which status is gauged, permitting men or women to marry into certain social milieux where they will feel that their degradation will be redeemed.

Need I remind you that the emotional and psychological reactions of the oppressed are bewildering in their complexity? It simply means that oppression oppresses, that oppression takes its toll, that it leaves a mark behind. Now there are Asians and Africans, American and West Indian Negroes, who will wish to deny that oppression cuts as sharply and deeply into their hearts as I've outlined. But their denial of this is in itself proof of its truth, for their denial of what they feel under oppression is proof that oppression oppresses.

"THE UNITY OF MAN"

Environmental buffetings, crass racial distinctions, class discriminations, uprootings caused by migration, continual disillusionments, imprisonment for rebellious acts—all these hammer blows need not always produce shattered or mangled personalities. Sifting through such grinding social sieves are some whose characters are singularly free and whose apprehension of life is broad indeed. (I'm not implying that mistreatment and injustice ennoble character! Adversity, at times, crushes as well as molds; it would seem that if there is a latent predilection toward meanness, pressure will heighten it, and, conversely, if there is a tendency toward breadth and scope of outlook, pressure can release or aid its development.) It has been almost only among Asians and Africans of an artistic stamp and whose background has consisted of wars, revolutions, and harsh colonial experience that I've found a sense of the earth belonging to, and being the natural home of, all the men inhabiting it, an attitude that went well beyond skin color, races, parties, classes, and nations. On the other hand, I've heard Western whites declare frequently and with firm conviction that they felt that Africa was for the blacks, Asia was for the yellows and browns, and that Europe was for the whites, meaning, of course, that the past domination of Europe over those Asian-African areas was natural and justified by the racial structure of life and history itself, since both have reflected, during the past five hundred years, the supremacy of whites.

Amid some Asian-African scholastic circles, I found that Western scientific thought had encouraged some rare men toward a healthy skepticism not only of Christianity, but toward all traditional ideas. Striking advances in the realms of anthropology and Freudian psychology have stressed not as much the old-time diversities among men that the colonials and nineteenth-century scientists loved to insist upon, but the remarkable and growing body of evidence of the basic emotional kinship, empirically established, of all men and of all races. Today many of the scholars of Asia and Africa (a minority, to be sure, for I've found that psychological facts do not sit well upon the mentalities of oppressed people!) are beginning to feel a lessening of distance between themselves and the Western world. Indeed, I'd say that there exists in a given number of Asian and African intellectuals a profounder grasp of the psychology of the white Westerner than you would find among a comparable number of Western intellectuals toward the Asian and African. It is amusing and instructive to hear a Westernized African poet say, with pardonable superiority and pride born of detached insight:

"They call us uncivilized. But just read a volume of psychoanalytic case histories of white people! All of the culture of so-called barbaric Africa is re-enacted on a couch in a psychoanalytic office when a New York white man pours out his dreams, paying $20 an hour for the honor of doing so. Our tribes say and do the same things each day for the fun of it."

In all fairness it must be emphasized that this as yet budding sense of "the unity of man" is confined to a minority of minorities; but, despite the fragility of this universal outlook, it indicates a political vista that needs must be mentioned here. The present leaders of the newly independent Asian-African states have come under daily and bitter criticism in the press of the Western world; they have been branded as "wild-eyed," "neutrals," "immoralists," and "unappreciative of the danger of Communism." What the Western press does not realize is that the delicately poised elite in these areas represents the only real bastions of Western thought beyond the confines of the West. If these few Western-minded leaders are overthrown, it is absolutely certain that their successors will be infinitely more anti-Western than they are. The closer the West approaches the Asian and African masses, the more exclusive, shy, evasive, and militantly racial and nationalistic it will find those masses to be. This is but another way of saying that the present Asian-African leadership is one that can continue to talk to the West in terms of Western concepts and within a Western frame of reference, no matter how many hot disputes may take place about ends and means.

I know that some romantic- and regressive-minded Westerners would prefer to deal with a more pliable and less intransigent Asian-African elite. But they will discover, to their sharp dismay, that this "softer" elite will have little or no influence over the illiterate masses who are still captured by their ancestral or mystical religious systems. Those Asian-African leaders who can grasp "the unity of man" are few, and the bare fact that there exist even a few possessing global and humane visions is really a kind of miracle (especially when one recalls the past recent history of the West in those areas!), a boon that the West should think hard upon before dismissing in disdain or racial scorn.

"LAY PRIESTS"

The Asian-African leader is often far more conscious of his relation to his people than a Westerner is to his. The non-Westerner knows that he is functionally the direct descendant of the priest, the mystic, the saint, the chief, "the fathers of the people." Hence, though ofttimes lacking official sanction for his position, he wields a kind of power that the Western mind finds difficult to grasp. A Nkrumah, a Nasser, a Nehru, all of whom hold official offices, speak with an authority that goes beyond the mandates of elections; indeed, the official posts which they now hold were gained only after they had conquered the hearts of their people. And these Asian-African stand-ins for priestly powers know that when they meet Western engineers, bankers, industrialists, scientists, etc., they are regarded with distrust, suspicion, if not the downright scorn that is reserved for "eggheads."

The most powerful public organs in Asia and Africa are often not government-sponsored bodies at all, but are, on the contrary, *government-creating bodies*—the Western procedure being turned upsidedown in non-Western countries. The "leader" and his movement exercise a power that is above that of law. And it is safe to assume that this quasi-religious atmosphere will prevail until more secular ground has been won from the traditional institutions and a body of pragmatic experience has accumulated in the daily lives of the people.

The role of Asian-African "lay priests" is extremely difficult and complicated; they function in a situation that facilitates the mischief-making efforts of their Communist competitors who seek to win converts at their expense, promising quicker results, inflaming class feelings long before the issue of national independence is resolved. Educated for the most part in Russia, speaking the language of the common people, enjoying the most intimate contacts with the masses, projecting their missionary ideas in terms of the people's daily lives, the Communist agitator fills a vacuum by rushing in where more prudent nationalists would hesitate. The Asian-African nationalist elite often finds itself in an odd position of having to battle a species of home-grown Communism on the one hand, and a futile striving to win Western understanding, approval, and support on the other. Many times it turns from both sides in desperation, with an attitude of: "A plague on both your houses."

"Post-Mortem Terror"

I'd like now to move towards a more minute examination of this question and I'd like to confine my remarks mainly to consciousness of the elite of Asia, Africa, and the West Indies, for it is in this elite, educated in the West, and, for the most part, more Western than the West, that the truly tragic aspects of oppression can be seen and measured. I know that it is popular today to say that every square inch of human existence is wholly economic. That is easy, too easy. It's a good organizing slogan, but it is no guide when it comes to examining and weighing the human issues and attitudes involved.

As the waters of Western imperialism recede from the land masses of Asia and Africa, and when we begin to study the residue left behind, we shall find some strange formations indeed. The first curious fact that I'd like to call to your attention is that, though recently freed, many lands—Indonesia, Ceylon, Burma, India, the Gold Coast—are more profoundly upset, filled with more fear and unrest than obtained even when the colonizing power was there in all of its brutal glory. Why is this? Why is Indonesia not only socially and economically disorganized, but emotionally and psychologically upset? I've called this strange state of mind: Post-Mortem Terror. What do I mean by that?

It is a state of mind of newly freed colonial peoples who feel that they will be resubjugated; that they are abandoned, that no new house of the heart is as yet made for them to enter. They know that they do not possess the necessary tools and arms to guarantee their freedom. Hence, their terror in freedom, their anxiety right after their liberation, is greater than when under the dominance of the superior Western power. Many people have misread this phenomenon and said that the people were unhappy because the Western white man had gone. How silly. Their unrest stems from a fear that the white man will come back, and from the cold void in which they are suspended. Of course, this acute unrest, this thrashing about for a new security, is mainly confined to the elite that can see and know what the issues and odds are.

"THE CONCEPT OF INTERFERENCE"

What is the burden of consciousness of this elite? It looks at
the powerful West and then looks at the weakness of its own
lands and feels that some dire and drastic move must be made to
equalize the situation. What move can they make? They wish to
do all those things that will make their lands the equal of the
Western lands, for only in that way can they feel safe. But what
does that involve? This elite, you must remember, lives sur-
rounded by powerful traditions stretching back into the remote
past. It knows that any move it makes to extend the area of industrialization will be passively resisted by those of their own people
who do not know the modern world as well as they do, who do
not feel their sense of urgency.

Hence, this Asian-African elite, in its state of what I've called
Post-Mortem Terror, wishes to *interfere* with the religion and traditions of its land and its people. They are impelled to interfere
quickly, drastically, decisively, and break the force of religion and
tradition and create secular ground for the building of rational
societies. But something holds them back. What is it? Two forces
hamper and hinder them. First, this elite was educated in the
West and has grown used to gradual methods of social evolution.
Second, the white Westerner stands looking critically at this new
elite and warns: "Don't act like fascists toward your own people!"

I wonder if the white Western world can appreciate this agony.
I've called it: "The Caul of Indecision."

"THE CAUL OF INDECISION"

Before this issue, the oppressed elite sweats. A man belonging
to this elite argues. He questions himself. He fears the return of
the West, yet he feels that he needs the West. I will cite a few
examples of how the elite seeks to solve this all important problem. In the United States just after World War I, Marcus Garvey
rose to leadership among the American Negroes and proposed the
creation of all-black nationalism based on color, racial pride; his

aim was to settle the American Negroes again in Africa and build an industrial state. His scheme failed mainly for two reasons: it was premature, and the Negroes in America felt themselves more psychologically identified with America than with Africa.

In the Gold Coast we see Nkrumah trying to forge tribes into a unity based on modern political concepts, and we can see today the degree to which his efforts clash bitterly, bloodily, with the traditions and ambitions of Ashanti tribal life. Whether Nkrumah will be successful or not only the future will tell. (He has so far been successful.) In Indonesia the new government under Sastroamidjojo* has called for compulsory national service in order to step up the rate of industrialization and rehabilitation. In India, Nehru has had to set the guns of his police against the reactionary claims of tribes whose outlook falls far behind that of the Western-educated elite. These actions are tragic. Where does the white West stand in this matter? With the tribes! With superstition! With the noble savage! Imagine! The West sides with the tribes against the men whom it educated. They now find the naked tribal man a noble, wonderful creature. How selfish can you get? The West has had five hundred years to protect those tribes. I say let the elite try a bit.

But let's examine this tragic conflict between the Western elite of Asia and Africa and their own populations. It can be stated without fear of contradiction that it would not exist if that elite did not have bitter memories and fears of the Western white man. The reason for this brutal push of the elite against its own people stems from fear that if they do not quickly modernize their countries, the white man will return. So, instead of democracy obtaining in the newly freed areas, something hinting of dictatorship will no doubt prevail for a while—will prevail at least until fear of the West has died down.

Listen to what Gunnar Myrdal, executive secretary of the Economic Commission for the United Nations, says:

---

*Since these lines were written, elective democracy has been suspended in Indonesia and a form of "guided" democracy has been enthroned in its place.

"If, as is assumed to be an urgent necessity in the underdeveloped countries, the movement toward industrialization is to be pushed ahead, the *state*[*] will have to intervene in the field of manufacturing . . . not only creating the external economies and supplying transport and power, but often also organizing the marketing of the produce of the expanding industrial sector, providing facilities for training workers, foremen, and technicians on all levels, as well as business executives, giving managerial advice, making capital available, often subsidizing or protecting new industrial enterprises, and sometimes actually establishing and operating them. At the same time it must have as its principal objective not only the development of industrialization to its practical limits, but also its direction, so that the growth is balanced and met by effective demand."

Sounds like the blueprint for a Soviet, huh? Is Gunnar Myrdal perverse in assigning so powerful a role to the state? Well, either plans like this are followed, or stagnation lingers on and bloody revolution comes. The road to freedom might well lead through stern mountain paths. And, mind you, Myrdal gives this advice to keep those men of the elite in Asia and Africa in the camp of democracy! Paradoxical, but it's true.

Did this notion of interfering with the lives of their own people stem from an innate cruelty on the part of the elite of Asia and Africa? No. And there's the joker. What this elite seeks to impose in Asia and Africa derives from the concepts they learned in Western schools. This elite learned how Europe, during the Reformation, had rolled back the tide of religion and had established the foundations of the modern state, secular institutions, free speech, science, etc. And what this Asian and African elite is now trying to do, under conditions far more difficult than obtained in Europe, is to rebuild their lands quickly, in terms of self-defense.

Do I make this point clear? The sense of urgency that rides the elite of Asia and Africa so desperately stems from a feeling that if

[*]My italics. R. W.

they do not measure up almost overnight, they will again be swallowed up in what they feel will be a new slavery. This was the fundamental mood of Bandung.

(Not long ago I had the opportunity to mention this widespread notion of interference to an audience in Paris, and some young man, imbued with absolutistic thought, rose and denounced me for advocating American intervention in Asia and Africa! Which goes to show how propaganda can mislead and blind people.)

"THE CULT OF SACRIFICE"

Let us follow this tragic theme of the elite a little more. Since the newly freed Asian and African nations do not possess enough technical power, they must needs often reckon their strength in terms of human sacrifices. Indeed, sacrifice, deliberate and intentional, has become a means of political struggle. One of the cardinal traits of the national revolutionary is to anticipate in advance the cost of the liberation of his land in terms of human life and physical suffering. Since he is faced with a Western world that stubbornly clings to the idea that God Himself has given it the right to rule the "lesser breed," the elite of Asia and Africa has no other choice but the embracing of this melancholy outlook, as depressing as it is.

It is to be noted that at Bandung President Sukarno pointed out in his opening address the role that sacrifice had played in the struggle against imperialist domination.

Indeed, this mentality of sacrifice lingers on even after the colonial area wins its freedom. In fact, in many instances the freed colonial subject will react in terms of his former situation. He feels that all his actions ought to carry punitive measures, penalties, so used has he grown to feeling and thinking of enduring chastisement for his rebellious acts. This almost masochistic tendency makes him rush forward to embrace all the threats that the white West could possibly hurl at him. Hence, military threats are discounted in their minds in advance. I found in Asia and Africa that the degree of suffering that a leader had under-

gone at the hands of Western whites was a definition of his standing as a hero. Mrs. Pandit told me at Bandung that it was the
years that Nehru had spent in jail that were now enabling Nehru
to hold the Hindu millions in a state of unity while the nation
was being rebuilt. In Indonesia some of the highest posts of government could be won only by those men who had a past record
of imprisonment. In the Gold Coast the party in power marched
into the National Assembly wearing the caps that they had worn
while behind jail bars.

But is all of this as negative as I have so far stated it? I've shown
more or less the reaction of the Asian and African to the white
West, its past domination and present pressures. Are there no positive elements of a psychological nature in this Asian-African reaction? There are indeed positive psychological motives. I shall
attempt to list some of them.

"THE NUCLEAR REVOLUTIONARY MOTIVE"

At the top of this list I shall place what I have called the
Nuclear Revolutionary Motive. Just what does this clumsy phrase
mean? I shall here try to spell out something that has gone
almost unnoticed in the Western world. What was the main
impact of the West upon Asia and Africa? I know that Marxists
will say that it was economic. Non-Marxists will say that it was
Christianity. Academic men will try to persuade us that there was
a mixture, a synthesis of East and West involved. Here, I propose
to advance another concept to account for this impact of the
West upon Asia and Africa, a concept that cuts down beneath
the other answers. I maintain that the ultimate effect of white
Europe upon Asia and Africa was to cast millions into a kind of
spiritual void; I maintain that it suffused their lives with a sense
of meaninglessness. I argue that it was not merely physical suffering or economic deprivation that has set over a billion and a half
colored people in violent political motion. I further maintain
that a mere class identification is not sufficient to describe manifestations such as Bandung, for it must be remembered that

modern class relations and proletarian class consciousness do not exist in many of the societies of Asia and Africa.

The present-day attitude of the national revolutionary in Asia and Africa has the quality of a man who has been put to sleep for centuries and awakens to find the world of which he was once a functioning part roaring past him. He is bewildered, hurt, stunned, filled with a sense of self-hate at the trick he feels has been played upon him. He and his kind are many; his adversaries are relatively few in number. The world that such a man sees is devoid of meaning. He looks into this or that theory to find an idea of what has happened to him and his kind. And when he selects a theory, whether it be Marxism or any other revolutionary doctrine, he is not so much concerned emotionally with whether that theory is *right* or *wrong,* but whether it fits his feelings and most nearly describes what he sees and feels. Does it fill that aching void in him? Indeed, I'll go so far as to say that, psychologically, theories here are but excuses, justifications, rationalizations for actions. Here we come to that strange frontier where we can say that motive becomes ideology.

Have I been understood? What I'm saying is this: I'm presenting you with a picture that turns the usual view of this matter upside down. I state that emotion here precedes the idea, that attitudes select the kind of ideas in question. This is the void that the West has induced in the Asian and African elite and the filling of that void is with ideas THAT MOST NEARLY ANSWER THE NEED. The idea that is accepted usually depends upon which idea gets there first!

The dynamic concept of the void that must be filled, a void created by a thoughtless and brutal impact of the West upon a billion and a half people, is more powerful than the concept of class conflict, and more universal.

I know that there are those of you who will bridle at this assertion. Perhaps you will feel that I'm devaluing the passion felt by national revolutionaries, and that I'm painting the Western white man as a brutal idiot. I'm not trying to do any such thing. I say that, upon sound reflection, if you get rid of some of your preconceptions, you will see that this concept of the void-to-be-filled can be equated to a *raison d'être,* a justification for living.

It is interesting to recall that Khrushchev's recent visit to India resulted in the Russian Communist leader's making a significant admission. He said that Gandhi had made a most important contribution to the national liberation struggle in India. Now, many of us had known that little fact for a long, long time, but it took a personal visit of Khrushchev to find it out. In India millions felt that the British method of rule was nullifying their very sense of life, and they, under Gandhi's guidance, organized to oppose it. What happened? Gandhi did not get what he wanted. He organized India to *resist* British industrialization and ironically he thereby launched India upon the road of industrialization. Gandhi was dealing with processes that far outstripped his own imagination.

Let me call to your attention some of the traits of this void in Asia and Africa.

"MEN WITHOUT LANGUAGE"

The elite of Asia and Africa are truly men without language. I do not mean that they do not speak their own native tongues; I do not mean that they do not speak the language of the European countries that dominated their lands for so long. It is psychological language that I speak of. For these men there is a "hole" in history, a storm in their hearts that they cannot describe, a stretch of centuries whose content has been interpreted only by white Westerners. The seizure of his country, its subjugation, the introduction of military rule, another language, another religion—all of these events existed without his interpretation of them. Even when he sends his children to school in Europe he knows that they will be taught his country's past in a manner that he disapproves. Put differently, one can say that at this point the elite has no vocabulary of history. What has happened to him is something about which he has yet to speak.

One day in Indonesia an educator and writer said to me:

"How I envy you."

"Why?" I asked him.

"The English language is your mother tongue," he told me.

"That's true," I said.

"You can appeal, as a writer, to a vast, world-wide audience," he went on.

"Yes," I agreed.

"But, Goddammit, they taught us *Dutch!*" he stormed. "What can I say in Dutch? To whom can I speak?"

He seethed. Both of us were historical victims of a sort. He had been taught Dutch and I had been taught English. This Indonesian writer and educator was leading the crusade for the rehabilitation of his old language, Bahasa Malay, as the national language of his country. This man felt it was preferable for his children to speak a language that would enable them to appeal eventually to seventy million Indonesians than to learn Dutch, which would allow them communication with nine million people in a tiny dull European country called Holland.

It is almost impossible for a white Westerner to realize some of the facts that make non-Westerners angry and resentful.

"THE ZONE OF SILENCE"

Ofttimes the elite is silent. There's a spell of quiet that comes over him when he sees that the point of view of the imperial power dominates the values of culture and life. The world confronting him negates his humanity, but he feels that it is useless to protest with words. Only a complete reversal of the economic and political situation can give him back his birthright, can enable him to speak, to allow him to grasp a language, a vocabulary, that he can feel is his own.

"THE STATE OF EXAGGERATION"

Obviously, any elite reacting to the kind of reality I've sketched here will find itself reacting violently. One of the aspects of life of the American Negro that has amazed observers is the emotional intensity with which he attacks ordinary, daily problems. When an American Negro tries to rent a house and is refused, he will react far more violently than a white who tries to rent the same house and is refused. Is this biological? No. The Negro can always feel that his refusal was based on color. The political rallies of the African Gold Coast reached an intensity of passion that actually frightened Europeans who did not realize that these political rallies were not just politics, but attempts at forging a new way of life. The devotion and fervor that characterized the organization at Bandung reduced Western observers to silence and fear. And the vast crowds that attended the recent Asian tour of Khrushchev and Bulganin rendered a homage to an industrialized Russia that was non-ideological in origin.

Is it not clear that we are dealing here with attitudes that go beyond a mere reacting to local or limited events? These reactions go beyond mere politics; they involve the total attitudes of the men concerned.

"RECOIL AND SELF-POSSESSION"

In many instances racists or colonial administrators justified their harsh methods on the grounds that, once their rule was lifted, there would be a disorganized and aggressive surge forward on the part of the black and brown and yellow men. In the American South, the white racists contended that, once all Jim Crow laws were repealed, the blacks would leap through windows and rape their wives and daughters. But, in Alabama, when the United States Supreme Court declared the Jim Crow practices on the buses unconstitutional, there was no wild rush forward on the part of the Alabama blacks. Instead, those blacks put forward a demand that they be allowed to organize and operate their own bus companies! In this instance, how could the whites have so completely misread the reality that lay so plainly in the black minds? On one hand, the whites had projected out upon the blacks their own guilt, fears, and sexual preoccupations. On the other, the blacks wished a respite from their bruising contacts with whites, sought a period in which they could take stock of what they really wanted.

In the Gold Coast the Britishers were always alarmed when the Africans went off by themselves to hold their political rallies and were constantly asking: "What did they say? What are they planning? Don't they want partnership?"

At Bandung the proud Australians were in the embarrassing position of chiding Indonesians and Indians and Africans for having excluded them from the greatest international conference that ever took place in Asia in modern times.

I've been informed by reliable international experts that in New Delhi the white ambassadors of European nations fret and fume because they do not have easy access to a tan-skinned Nehru who spent a third of his adult life in prison under white jailers.

Because I've pointed out these tendencies to recoil and self-possession on the part of Asians and Africans, some critics have sought to brand me a racist. This is a primitive reaction and is akin to accusing a messenger who brings you bad news of having created the bad news he brings.

This Asian-African recoil and withdrawal have many determinations, the most distinctive and powerful of which is to reorganize their lives in accordance with their own basic feelings. The truncated religious structure comes again to the fore and reasserts itself, much to the astonishment of Europeans. The conference of black artists and writers recently concluded in Paris by *Présence Africaine* is a vivid example of this stocktaking on the part of the elite of the black world. It is a recoil and withdrawal prompted by psychological necessity, but it is far from being a negative gesture. It is a regrouping of psychological forces for constructive action—psychological forces that have been scattered and paralyzed for centuries.

The last psychological aspect I'd like to discuss with you shall be under the listing of:

"The Mystique of Numbers"

Lacking modern techniques and arms to secure them from invasion or resubjugation, the newly freed Asian and African elite shies off from the urgent and insistent suggestion of white Western social scientists to limit, reduce, or control their populations. We all know that modern medicines, modern methods of sanitation, and new techniques of production enable tropical populations to increase so rapidly that they quickly outstrip the capacity of the means of production—even when those means of production are being aided by outside forces. But when Westerners urge birth control and other methods of limiting populations upon Asians and Africans, they are heard with considerable reserve. I propose to discuss, however briefly, some of the psychological motives back of that reserve.

The most powerful element here, of course, is the religious background of Asia and Africa, a background of worshipful regard for ancestors. Children are not only new members of the community, but are viewed in the light of reincarnations of past family members. Hence, the Asian or African is likely to listen with a poker face to the white social scientist when he argues passionately for a reduction or a limitation of the population of his country.

Facing superior arms, the Asian-African elite is likely to feel that, the more of his kind there is around him, the better off he is. And, as the white social scientist points out the advantages in terms of higher standards of living that will accrue if he limits his population, the Asian or African will ask himself uneasily: "Why does he wish that we were not so numerous?"

The Asian-African suspects bad faith in this argument, and I believe that he is right. It can be argued that the West is ethically dubious when it urges upon Asians and Africans concepts or principles that the West discovered only accidentally and under conditions far different from those that obtain in Asia and Africa.

It is well-known that the populations of the West are relatively smaller than those of Asia and Africa. But those low populations of the West did not come about through deliberate efforts on the part of the West. They were the consequences of complicated social, economic, and cultural factors. It would be safe to say that there will be no limiting or control of Asian or African populations until there prevail in Asia and Africa more or less the same conditions that obtain in the West. And, when that time comes, there will be no need for Western social scientists to urge a reduction of populations upon Asian and African leaders.

An examination of the population problem will reveal a common attitude existing among all people apprehensive about their future and afraid of attack. The Russians boast of their 200 million. The Chinese boast of their 600 million.* Africa is proud of her 170 million. At Bandung no delegate rose to speak without paying tribute to the fact that the conference represented a billion and a half people. It can be seen that population here is regarded in the light of a protective weapon.

We have been tramping through an unknown country. In this chapter I've tried to indicate the main peaks and valleys. This listing of psychological reactions is by no means complete. In raising this subject I'm trying to spur others to plunge in and make explorations.

Psychological facts have about them an air of the derogatory. But this is only seemingly so. You must realize that what I've called Asian and African psychological facts are such only in a contingent sense. They are human reactions, and, as such, they belong to everybody. White men under the conditions I've described would have reacted more or less the same. I have not raised these questions in order to deny, demean, or criticize the reactions I've cited. These reactions are human, all too human.

I challenge Europe to be strong enough to admit and accept this revolution that she cast into the world, however unconsciously, stupidly, misguidedly, and clumsily she did it. Like a

---

*In the torrid political debates of Hindus, Chinese, Africans, and Indonesians that rage in the cafés of Paris, one hears the frequent and defiantly masochistic declaration: "China could fight a war for twenty years and lose twenty million men and *still* have a population of six hundred million left!"

sleepwalker, Europe blundered into the house of mankind, nullifying ancient traditions that sustained and informed the lives of
millions with meaning, shattering the mental crystallizations of
centuries and sending black, brown, and yellow men hurtling
toward horizons as yet distant and dim. The Western world has,
through sheer selfishness and racial jealousy, lost a vital part of
this revolution to Communism, for, when called upon to confess
authorship of her own principles, she rejected them and called
them forgeries.

The historical hour is late, too late for guns, too late for armies
even. If we would have a free world, only an awakened and chas-
tened Europe can sanction it, can give the word. Europe must
admit the role she has played in history, the noble as well as the
base aspects of that role. Europe must be big enough to accept its
Descartes and its Cortés and what they did. Europe must be big
enough to accept its Hume of England and its Leopold II of
Belgium and what they did. It must possess enough stern responsibility to accept both its Goethe and its Hitler. Is the spirit of
Europe big enough to admit and contain and resolve these contradictions? If it is, our world can be saved. If it is not, our world
is lost. And the world that we save or lose is a bigger world than
we are, and our last one.

It can be said that the white man is at bay. Never have so few
hated and feared so many. What I dread is that the Western white
man, confronted with an implacably militant Communism on
the one hand, and with a billion and a half colored people
gripped by surging tides of nationalist fanaticism on the other,
will feel that only a vengeful unleashing of atom and hydrogen
bombs can make him feel secure. I dread that there will be an
attempt at burning up millions of people to make the world safe
for the "white man's" conception of existence, to make the ideas
of Mill and Hume and Locke good for all people, at all times,
everywhere. There is no doubt that atom or hydrogen bombs can
destroy much of human life on this earth. If the white West
should attack the body of mankind in this fashion, it will not
only sacrifice its own civilization, but will set off reactions of

racial and religious hatreds that will last for generations. In trying in this manner to make the world safe for their own kind only, the white West will wipe out of men's minds the undoubtedly glorious contributions that it has made to human life on this earth. In that instance, the only possible winner can be Communism. And if Communism wins under such stupid conditions, its victory will have been given to it by the racial jealousies of the Western world, jealousies which make the West feel that it would rather have no world at all than to share it, living and letting live, giving and taking.

2

Tradition and Industrialization

THE HISTORIC MEANING OF THE PLIGHT OF THE TRAGIC ELITE IN ASIA AND AFRICA

So great a legion of ideological interests is choking the media of communication of the world today that I deem it advisable to define the terms in which I speak and for whom. In the heated, charged, and violently partisan atmosphere in which we live at this moment, all public utterances are dragged willy-nilly into the service of something or somebody. Even the most rigorously determined attitudes of objectivity and the most passionate avowals of good faith have come to be suspect. And especially is this true of the expressions of those of us who have been doomed to live and act in a tight web of racial and economic facts, facts viewed by many through eyes of political or religious interest, facts examined by millions with anxiety and even hysteria.

Knowing the suspicious, uneasy climate in which our twentieth-century lives are couched, I, as a Western man of color, strive to be as objective as I can when I seek to communicate. But, at once, you have the right to demand of me: What does being objective mean? Is it possible to speak at all today and not have the meaning of one's words construed in six different ways?

For example, he who advocates the use of mass educational techniques today can be, and usually is, accused of harboring secret Soviet sympathies, despite the fact that his advocacy of the means of mass education aims at a quick spreading of literacy so that Communism cannot take root, so that vast populations trapped in tribal or religious loyalties cannot be easily duped by self-seeking demagogues. He who urgently counsels the establishment of strong, central governments in the so-called underdeveloped countries, in the hope that those countries can quickly pull themselves out of the mire and become swiftly modernized and industrialized and thereby set upon the road to democracy, free speech, a secular state, universal suffrage, etc., can be and commonly is stigmatized as: "Well, he's no Communist, *but* . . ." He who would invoke, as sanction for experimental political action, a desire to seek the realization of the basic ideals of the Western world in terms of unorthodox and as yet untried institutional structures—instrumentalities for short-cutting long, drawn-out historical processes—as a means of constructing conditions for the creation of individual freedom, can be branded as being "emotionally unstable and having tendencies that *could* lead, therefore, to Communism." He who would question, with all the good faith in the world, whether the philosophical ideas and assumptions of John Stuart Mill and John Locke are valid for all times, for all peoples, and for all countries with their vastly differing traditions and backgrounds, with the motive of psychologically freeing men's minds so that they can seek new conditions and instrumentalities for freedom, can be indicted as an enemy of democracy.

Confronted with a range of negative hostility of this sort, knowing that the society of the Western world is so frantically defensive that it would seek to impose conformity at any price, what is an honest man to do? Should he keep silent and thereby try to win a degree of dubious safety for himself? Should he endorse static defensiveness as the price of achieving his own personal security? The game isn't worth the candle, for, in doing so, he buttresses that which would eventually crush not only him, but that which would negate the very conditions of life out of which freedom can spring. In such a situation one's silence implies that one has surrendered one's intellectual faculties to fear, that one had voluntarily abdicated life itself, that one has gratuitously paralyzed one's possibilities of action. Since any and all events can be lifted by men of bad faith out of their normal contexts and projected into others and thus consequently condemned, since one's thoughts can be interpreted in terms of such extreme implications as to reduce them to absurdity or subversion, obviously a mere declaration of one's good intentions is not enough. In an all-pervading climate of intellectual evasion or dishonesty, everything becomes dishonest; suspicion subverts events and distorts their meaning; mental reservations alter the character of facts and rob them of validity and utility. In short, if good will is lacking, everything is lost and a dialogue between men becomes not only useless, but dangerous, and sometimes even incriminating.

To imagine that straight communication is no longer possible is to declare that the world we seek to defend is no longer worth defending, that the battle for human freedom is already lost. I'm assuming, however naively, that such is not quite yet the case. I cannot, of course, assume that universal good will reigns, but I have the elementary right, the bounden duty even, to assume that man, when he has the chance to speak and act without fear, still wishes to be man, that is, he harbors the dream of being a free and creative agent.

Then, first of all, let us honestly admit that there is no such thing as objectivity, no such objective fact as objectivity. Objectivity is a fabricated concept, a synthetic intellectual construction devised to enable others to know the general conditions under which one has done something, observed the world or an event in that world.

So, before proceeding to give my opinions concerning Tradition and Industrialization, I shall try to state as clearly as possible where I stand, the mental climate about me, the historic period in which I speak, and some of the elements in my environment and my own personality which propel me to communicate. The basic assumption behind all so-called objective attitudes is this: If others care to assume my mental stance and, through empathy, duplicate the atmosphere in which I speak, if they can imaginatively grasp the factors in my environment and a sense of the impulses motivating me, they will, if they are of a mind to, be able to see, more or less, what I've seen, will be capable of apprehending the same general aspects and tones of reality that comprise my world, that world that I share daily with all other men. By revealing the assumptions behind my statements, I'm striving to convert you to my outlook, to its essential humaneness, to the generality and reasonableness of my arguments.

Obviously no striving for an objectivity of attitude is ever complete. Tomorrow, or the day after, someone will discover some fact, some element, or a nuance that I've forgotten to take into account, and, accordingly, my attitude will have to be revised, discarded, or extended, as the case may be. Hence, there is no such thing as an absolute objectivity of attitude. The most rigorously determined attitude of objectivity is, at best, relative. We are human; we are the slaves of our assumptions, of time and circumstance; we are the victims of our passions and illusions; and the most that our critics can ask of us is this: Have you taken your passions, your illusions, your time, and your circumstances into account? That is what I am attempting to do. More than that no reasonable man of good will can demand.

First of all, my position is a split one. I'm black. I'm a man of the West. These hard facts are bound to condition, to some degree, my outlook. I see and understand the West; but I also see and understand the non- or anti-Western point of view. How is this possible? This double vision of mine stems from my being a product of Western civilization and from my racial identity, long and deeply conditioned, which is organically born of my being a product of that civilization. Being a Negro living in a white Western Christian society, I've never been allowed to blend, in a natural and healthy manner, with the culture and civilization of the West. This contradiction of being both Western and a man of color creates a psychological distance, so to speak, between me and my environment. I'm self-conscious. I admit it. Yet I feel no need to apologize for it. Hence, though Western, I'm inevitably critical of the West. Indeed, a vital element of my Westernness resides in this chronically skeptical, this irredeemably critical, outlook. I'm restless. I question not only myself, but my environment. I'm eager, urgent. And to be so seems natural, human, and good to me. Life without these qualities is inconceivable, less than human. In spite of myself, my imagination is constantly leaping ahead and trying to reshape the world I see (basing itself strictly on the materials of the world in which I live each day) toward a form in which all men could share my creative restlessness. Such an outlook breeds criticism. And my critical attitude and detachment are born of my position. I and my environment are one, but that oneness has in it, at its very core, an abiding schism. Yet I regard my position as natural, as normal, though others, that is, Western whites, anchored in tradition and habit, would have to make a most strenuous effort of imagination to grasp it.

Yet, I'm not non-Western. I'm no enemy of the West. Neither am I an Easterner. When I look out upon those vast stretches of this earth inhabited by brown, black, and yellow men—sections of the earth in which religion dominates, to the exclusion of almost everything else, the emotional and mental landscape—my reactions and attitudes are those of the West. I see both worlds from another and third point of view. (This outlook has nothing to do with any so-called Third Force; I'm speaking largely in historical and psychological terms.)

I'm numbed and appalled when I know that millions of men in Asia and Africa assign more reality to their dead fathers than to

the crying claims of their daily lives: poverty, political degradation, illness, ignorance, etc. I shiver when I learn that the infant
mortality rate, say, in James Town (a slum section of Accra, the
capital of the Gold Coast in British West Africa) is fifty per cent
in the first year of life; and, further, I'm speechless when I learn
that this inhuman condition is explained by the statement, "The
children did not wish to stay. Their ghost-mothers called them
home." And when I hear that explanation I know that there can
be no altering of social conditions in those areas until such religious rationalizations have been swept from men's minds, no matter how devoutly they are believed in or defended. Indeed, the
teeming religions gripping the minds and consciousness of Asians
and Africans offend me. I can conceive of no identification with
such mystical visions of life that freeze millions in static degradation, no matter how emotionally satisfying such degradation
seems to those who wallow in it. But, because the swarming populations in those continents are two-time victims—victims of
their own religious projections and victims of Western imperialism—my sympathies are unavoidably with, and unashamedly for,
them. For this sympathy I offer no apology.

Yet, when I turn to face the environment that cradled and nurtured me, I experience a sense of dismaying shock, for that
Western environment is soaked in and stained with the most blatant racism that the contemporary world knows. It is a racism
that has almost become another kind of religion, a religion of the
materially dispossessed, of the culturally disinherited. Rooted in
my own disinheritedness, I know instinctively that this clinging
to, and defense of, racism by Western whites are born of their
psychological nakedness, of their having, through historical accident, partially thrown off the mystic cauls of Asia and Africa that
once too blinded and dazed them. A deeply conscious victim of
white racism could even be strangely moved to compassion for
that white man who, having lost his mystic vision of a stern
Father God, a dazzling Virgin, and a Dying Son Who promises to
succor him after death, settles upon racism! What a poor substitute! What a shabby, vile, and cheap home the white heart finds

when it seeks shelter in racism! One would think that sheer pride would deter Western whites from such emotional debasement!

I stand, therefore, mentally and emotionally looking in both directions, being claimed by a negative identification on one side, and being excluded by a feeling of repulsion on the other.

Since I'm detached from, because of racial conditions, the West, why do I bother to call myself Western at all? What is it that prompts me to make an identification with the West despite the contradiction involved? The fact is that I really have no choice in the matter. Historical forces more powerful than I am have shaped me as a Westerner. I have not consciously elected to be a Westerner; I have been made into a Westerner. Long before I had the freedom to choose, I was molded a Westerner. It began in childhood. And the process continues.

Hence, standing shoulder to shoulder with the Western white man, speaking his tongue, sharing his culture, participating in the common efforts of the Western community, I say frankly to that white man: "I'm Western, just as Western as you are, maybe more, but I don't completely agree with you."

What do I mean, then, when I say that I'm Western? I shall try to define what the term means to me. I shan't here, now, try to define what being Western means to all Westerners. I shall confine my definition only to that aspect of the West with which I identify, that aspect that makes me feel, act, and live Western.

The content of my Westernness resides fundamentally, I feel, in my secular outlook upon life. I believe in a separation of Church and State. I believe that the State possesses a value in and for itself. I feel that man—just sheer brute man, just as he is—has a meaning and value over and above all sanctions or mandates from mystical powers, either on high or from below. I am convinced that the humble, fragile dignity of man, buttressed by a tough-souled pragmatism, implemented by methods of trial and error, can sufficiently sustain and nourish human life, can endow it with ample and durable meaning. I believe that all ideas have a right to circulate in the market place without restriction. I believe that all men should have the right to have their say without fear of the political "powers that be," without having to dread the punitive measures or the threat of invisible forces which some castes of men claim as their special domain—men such as priests and churchmen. (My own position compels me to grant those priests and churchmen the right to have their say, but not at the expense of having my right to be heard annulled.) I believe that art has its own autonomy, a self-sufficiency that extends beyond, and independent of, the spheres of political or priestly power or sanction. I feel that science exists without any a priori or metaphysical assumptions. I feel that human personality is an end in and for itself. In short, I believe that man, for good or ill, is his own ruler, his own sovereign, his own keeper. I hold human freedom as a supreme right and good for all men, my conception of freedom being the right of all men to exercise their natural and acquired powers as long as the exercise of those powers does not hinder others from doing the same.

These are my assumptions, my values, my morality, if you insist upon that word. Yet I hold these values at a time in history when they are threatened. I stand in the middle of that most fateful of all the world's centuries: the twentieth century. Nuclear energy, the center of the sun, is in the hands of men. In most of the land mass of Asia and Africa the traditional and customary class relations of feudal, capitalistic societies have been altered, frequently brutally shattered, by murder and terror. Most of the governments of the earth today rule, by one pretext or another, by open or concealed pressure upon the individual, by black lists, intimidation, fiat, secret police, and machine guns. Among intellectual circles the globe over the desperate question has been raised: "What is man?" In the East as in the West, wealth and the means of production have been taken out of private hands, families, clans, and placed at the disposal of committees and state bureaucrats. The consciousness of most men on earth is filled with a sense of shame, of humiliation, of memories of past servitude and degradation—and a sense of fear that that condition of servitude and degradation will return. The future for most men is an apprehensive void which has created the feeling that it has to be impetuously, impulsively filled, given a new content at all costs. With the freeing of Asia and most of Africa from Western rule, more active and unbridled religion now foments and agitates the minds and emotions of men than at any time since 1455! Man's world today lies in the pythonlike coils of vast irrational forces which he cannot control. This is the mental climate out of which I speak, a climate that tones my being and pitches consciousness on a certain plane of tension. These are the conditions under which I speak, conditions that condition me.

Now, the above assumptions and facts would and do color my view of history, that record of the rise and fall of traditions and religions. All of those past historical forces which have, accidentally or intentionally, helped to create the basis of freedom in human life, I extol, revere, and count as my fervent allies. Those conditions of life and history which thwart, threaten, and degrade the values and assumptions I've listed, I reject and consider harmful, something to be doggedly resisted.

Now, I'm aware that to some tender, sensitive minds such a decalogue of beliefs is chilling, arid, almost inhuman. And especially is this true of those multitudes inhabiting the dense, artistically cluttered Catholic countries of present-day Europe. To a richly endowed temperament such a declaration is akin to an invitation to empty out all the precious values of the past; indeed, to many millions such a declaration smacks of an attack upon what they have been taught to consider and venerate as civilization itself. The emotionally thin-skinned cannot imagine, even in the middle of our twentieth century, a world without external emotional props to keep them buttressed to a stance of constant meaning and justification, a world filled with overpowering mother and father and child images to anchor them in emotional security, to keep a sense of the warm, intimate, sustaining influence of the family alive. And I can readily conceive of such temperaments willing to condemn my attitude as being barbarian, willful, or perverse. What such temperaments do not realize is that my decalogue of beliefs does not imply that I've turned my back in scorn upon the past of mankind in so crude or abrupt a manner as they feel or think. Men who can slough off the beautiful mythologies, the enthralling configurations of external ceremonies, manners, and codes of the past are not necessarily unacquainted with, or unappreciative of, them; they have *interiorized* them, have reduced them to mental traits, psychological problems. I know, however, that such a fact is small comfort to those who love the past, who long to be caught up in rituals that induce blissful self-forgetfulness, and who would find the meaning of their lives in them. I confess frankly that I cannot solve this problem for everybody; I state further that it is my profound conviction that emotional independence is a clear and distinct human advance, a gain for all mankind and, if that gain and advance seem inhuman, there is nothing that can rationally be done about it. Freedom needs no apology.

Naturally, a man holding such values will view history in a rather novel light. How do these values compel me to regard the claims of Western imperialism? What virtue or evil do I assign to the overrunning of Asia and Africa by Western Christian white men? What about color prejudice? What about the undeniable technical and industrial power and superiority of the white West? How do I feel about the white man's vaunted claim—and I'm a product, reluctant, to be sure, of that white man's culture and civilization—that he has been called by his God to rule the world and to have all overriding considerations over the rest of mankind, that is, colored men?

And, since the Christian religion, by and large, has tacitly endorsed racism by the nature of its past historical spread and its present sway, how do I view that religion whose irrational core can propel it toward such ends, whether that religion be in Europe, Asia, or Africa? And, since tradition is generally but forms of frozen or congealed religion, how do I regard tradition?

I've tried to lead you to my angle of vision slowly, step by step, keeping nothing back. If I insist over and over again upon the personal perspective, it is because my weighing of external facts is bound organically with that personal perspective. My point of view is a Western one, but a Western one that conflicts at several vital

points with the present, dominant outlook of the West. Am I
ahead of or behind the West? My personal judgment is that I'm
ahead. And I do not say that boastfully; such a judgment is
implied by the very nature of those Western values that I hold dear.

Let me dig deeper into my personal position. I was born a
black Protestant in that most racist of all the American states:
Mississippi. I lived my childhood under a racial code, brutal and
bloody, that white men proclaimed was ordained of God, said
was made mandatory by the nature of their religion. Naturally, I
rejected that religion and would reject any religion which pre-
scribes for me an inferior position in life; I reject that tradition
and any tradition which proscribes my humanity. And, since the
very beginnings of my life on this earth were couched in this contradiction, I became passionately curious as to why Christians felt
it imperative to practice such wholesale denials of humanity. My
seeking carried me back to a crucial point in Western history
where a clearly enunciated policy on the part of the Church spelt
my and others' doom. In 1455 the Pope divided the world
between Spain and Portugal and decreed that those two nations
had not only the right, but the consecrated duty of converting or
enslaving all infidels. Now, it just so happened that at that time
all the infidels, from the white Western Christian point of view,
were in Asia, Africa, the many islands of the Atlantic, the Pacific,
and the then unknown Americas—and it just so happened that
they were all people of color.

Further reading of history brought me abreast of a strong
countercurrent of opposition to that Church that had imperialis-
tically condemned all colored mankind. When I discovered that
John Calvin and Martin Luther were stalwart rebels against the
domination of a Church that had condemned and damned the
majority of the human race, I felt that the impulses, however confused, animating them were moving in the direction of a fuller
concept of human dignity and freedom. But the Protestantism of
Calvin and Luther did not go far enough; they underestimated
the nature of the revolution they were trying to make. Their fight
against the dead weight of tradition was partial, limited. Racism

was historically and circumstantially embedded in their rejection of the claims of the Church that they sought to defeat. Calvin and Luther strove for freedom, but it was inevitably and inescapably only for their kind, that is, European whites. So, while recognizing the positive but limited nature of Calvin's and Luther's contribution, I had to look elsewhere for a concept of man that would not do violence to my own concept of, and feeling for, life.

What did magnetize me toward the emotional polarizations of Calvin and Luther was the curious psychological strength that they unknowingly possessed, a strength that propelled them, however clumsily, toward the goal of emotional independence. These two bold European insurgents had begun, though they called it by another name, a stupendous *introjection* of the religious symbols by which the men of their time lived. They were proponents of that tide that was moving from simple, naive credence toward self-skepticism, from a state of sensual slavery to the sights, sounds, and colors of the external world toward a stance of detachment. By some quirk of mental strength, they felt stronger than their contemporaries and could doubt and even doff the panoply of religious rituals and ceremonies and could either live without much of them or could, gropingly to be sure, stand psychologically alone to an amazing degree. In the lives of Calvin and Luther there had begun a dual process: on one hand, the emptying of human consciousness of its ancient, infantile, subjective accretions, and, on the other, a denuding of an anthropocentric world of the poetry that man had projected upon it. A two-way doubt of the world and of man's own self had set in, and this putting man and his world in question would not pause until it had enthroned itself in a new consciousness. Western man was taking that first step toward a new outlook that would not terminate until it had flowered in the bleak stretches of an undiscovered America which, ironically, was peopled by red-skinned "savages" who could not dream of doubting their own emotions or questioning the world that impinged upon their sensibilities. (The partially liberated Pilgrims slew those religiously captured "savages"!) Not understanding the implications of the needs prompting them, Calvin and Luther did not realize that what they were trying to do had already been neatly, clearly, and heroically done before by the brave and brooding Greeks who, overwhelmed by contradictory experiences and the antinomic currents of their own passions, had lifted their dazed eyes toward an empty Heaven and uttered those bitterly tragic words that were to become the motto of abandoned Western man:

"What do we do now?"

The Protestant is a queer animal who has never fully understood himself, has never guessed that he is an abortive freeman, an issue of historical birth that never quite came to full life. It has been conveniently forgotten that the Protestant is a product and a result of *oppression,* which might well account for his inability to latch directly onto the Greek heritage and thereby save himself a lot of useless and stupid thrashing about in history. Stripped by the heavy, intolerant conditions of Catholic rule of much of his superfluous emotional baggage, the emerging Protestant rebel, harassed by his enemies and haunted by his own guilt, was doomed to *react* rather than *act*, to *protest* rather than *affirm,* never fully grasping what was motivating him until he had been swept by history so far beyond his original problem that he had forgotten its initial content of meaning. The Protestant was being called to a goal the terrifying nature of which he had neither the courage nor the strength to see or understand. The Protestant is the brave blind man cursed by destiny with a burden which he has not the inner grace to accept wholeheartedly.

The ultimate consequences of Calvin's and Luther's rebellious doctrines and seditious actions, hatched and bred in emotional confusion, unwittingly created the soil out of which grew something that Calvin and Luther did not dream of. (And this is not the last time that I shall call your attention to an odd characteristic of the Western world; the men of the West seem prone in their actions to achieve results that contradict their motives. They have a genius for calling things by wrong names; they seek to save souls and become involved in murder; they attempt to enthrone God as an absolute and they achieve the establishment of the prerequisites of science and atheistic thought; they seem wedded to a terribly naive and childlike outlook upon the world and themselves, and they are filled with consternation when their actions produce results that they did not foresee.) Determined to plant the religious impulse in each individual's heart, declaring that each man could stand face to face with God, Calvin and Luther blindly let loose mental and emotional forces which, in turn, caused a vast revolution in the social, cultural, governmental, and economic conditions under which Western man lived—a revolution that finally negated their own racial attitudes! The first and foremost of these conditions were the guaranteeing of individual conscience and judgment, an act which loosened, to a degree, the men of Europe from custom and tradition, from the dead hand of the past, evoking a sense of future expectation, infinitely widening man's entire horizon. And yet this was achieved by accident! That's the irony of it. Calvin and Luther, preoccupied with metaphysical notions, banished dread from men's minds and allowed them to develop that courageous emotional strength which sanctioned and spurred the amassing of a vast heap of positive fact relating to daily reality. As a result of Calvin's and Luther's heresy, man began to get a grip upon his external environment. Science and industry were born and, through their rapid growth, each enriched the other and nullified the past notions of social structures, negated norms of nobility, of tradition, of priestly values, and fostered new social classes, new occupations, new experiences, new structures of government, new pleasures, hungers, dreams, in short, a whole new and unheard of universe. A Church world was transformed into a worldly world, any man's world, a world in which even black, brown, and yellow men could have the possibility to live and breathe.

Yet, while living with these facts, Europeans still believed in and practiced a racism that the very logic of the world they were creating told them was irrational and insane!

Buttressed by their belief that their God had entrusted the earth into their keeping, drunk with power and possibility, waxing rich through trade in commodities, human and non-human, with awesome naval and merchant marines at their disposal, their countries filled with human debris anxious for any adventures, psychologically armed with new facts, white Western Christian civilization, with a long, slow, and bloody explosion, hurled itself upon the sprawling masses of humanity in Asia and Africa.*

Perhaps now you'll expect me to pause and begin a vehement and moral denunciation of Europe. No. The facts are complex. In that process of Europe's overrunning of the rest of mankind a most bewildering mixture of motives, means, and ends took place. White men, spurred by religious and areligious motives—that is, to save the souls of a billion or so heathens and to receive the material blessings of God while doing so—entered areas of the earth where religion ruled with an indigenous absoluteness that did not even obtain in Europe.

Are we here confronted with a simple picture of virtue triumphing over villainy, of right over wrong, of the superior over the inferior, of the biologically fit blond beast over biologically botched brown, yellow, and black men? That is what Europe felt about it. But I do not think that that is a true picture of what really happened. Again I call your attention to the proneness of white Europe, under the influence of a strident, romantic individualism, to do one thing and call that thing by a name that no one but itself could accept or recognize.

What, then, happened? Irrationalism met irrationalism. The irrationalism of Europe met the irrationalism of Asia and Africa, and the resulting confusion has yet to be unraveled and understood. Europe called her adventure imperialism, the spread of civilization, missions of glory, of service, of destiny even. Asians and Africans called it colonization, blood-sucking, murder, butchery, slavery. There is no doubt that both sides had some measure of truth in their claims. But I state that neither side quite knew what was happening and neither side was conscious of the real process that was taking place. The truth lay beyond the blurred ken of both the European and his Asian and African victim.

*See The Psychological Reactions of Oppressed People.

I have stated publicly, on more than one occasion, that the economic spoils of European imperialism do not bulk so large or important to me. I know that today it is the fashion to list the long and many economic advantages that Europe gained from its brutal and bloody impact upon hundreds of millions of Asians and Africans. The past fifty years have created a sprawling literature of the fact that the ownership of colonies paid princely dividends. I have no doubt of it. Yet that fact does not impress me as much as still another and more obscure and more important fact. What rivets my attention in this clash of East and West is that an irrational Western world helped, unconsciously and unintentionally to be sure, to smash the irrational ties of religion and custom and tradition in Asia and Africa. THIS, IN MY OPINION, IS THE CENTRAL HISTORIC FACT! The European said that he was saving souls, yet he kept himself at a distance from the brown, black, and yellow skins that housed the souls that he claimed that he so loved and so badly wanted to save. Thank the white man's God for that bit of racial and color stupidity! His liberating effect upon Asia and Africa would not have been so thorough had he been more human.

Yes, there were a few shrewd Europeans who wanted the natives to remain untouched, who wished to see what they called the "nobility" of the black, brown, and yellow lives remain intact. The more backward and outlandish the native was, the more the European loved him. This attitude can be boiled down to one simple wish: The imperialist wanted the natives to sleep on in their beautifully poetic dreams so that the ruling of them could be more easily done. They devised systems of administration called "indirect rule," "assimilation," "gradual constitutional government," etc., but they all meant one simple thing; a white man's military peace, a white man's political order, and a white man's free trade, whether that trade involved human bodies or tin or oil.

Again, I say that I do not denounce this. Had even the white West known what it was really doing, it could not have done a better job of beginning to launch the liberation of the masses of Asia and Africa from their age-old traditions.

Being ignorant of what they were really doing, the men of Europe failed to fill the void that they were creating in the very heart of mankind, thereby compounding their strange historical felony.

There are Europeans today who look longingly and soulfully at the situation developing in the world and say: "But, really, we love 'em. We are friends of theirs!" To attitudes like that I can only say: "My friends, look again. Examine the heritage you left behind. Read the literature that your fathers and your fathers' fathers wrote about those natives. Your fathers were naive but honest men."

How many souls did Europe save? To ask that question is to make one laugh! Europe was tendering to the great body of mankind a precious gift which she, in her blindness and ignorance, in her historical shortsightedness, was not generous enough to give her own people! Today, a *knowing* black, brown, or yellow man can say:

"Thank you, Mr. White Man, for freeing me from the rot of my irrational traditions and customs, though you are still the victim of your irrational customs and traditions!"

There was a boon wrapped in that gift of brutality that the white West showered upon Asia and Africa. Over the centuries, meticulously, the white men took the sons and daughters of the chiefs and of the noble houses of Asia and Africa and instilled in them the ideas of the West so the eventual Westernized Asian and African products could become their collaborators. Yet they had no thoughts of how those Westernized Asians and Africans would fare when cast, like fishes out of water, back into their poetic cultures. (These unemployed Asians and Africans eventually became national revolutionaries, of course!) Shorn of all deep-seated faiths, these Westernized Asians and Africans had to sink or swim with no guides, no counsel. Over and above this, the Europeans launched vast industrial enterprises in almost all of the lands that they controlled, vast enterprises that wrought profound alterations in the Asian-African ways of life and thought. *In sum, white Europeans set off a more deep-going and sudden revolution in*

Asia and Africa than had ever obtained in all of the history of Europe. And they did this with supreme confidence. On one occasion Christian English gentlemen chartered a royal company for one thousand years to buy and sell black slaves! Oh, what hope they had!

I declare that merely rational motives could not have sustained the white men who damaged and destroyed the ancient Asian-African cultures and social structures; they had perforce to believe that they were the tools of cosmic powers, that they were executing the will of God, or else they would not have had the cruel daring to try to harness the body of colored mankind into their personal service. The sheer magnitude of their depredations and subjugations ought to have given them pause, but it never did to any effective degree. Only a blind and ignorant militancy could have sustained such insane ventures, such outlandish dreams. Indeed, one could say that it was precisely because the white Westerner had partially lost his rooting in his own culture that he could remain so insensitive to the dangerous unleashing of human forces of so vast and catastrophic a sweep. Had he been more at home in his own world of values, sheer prudence would have made him quail before the earth-shaking human energies which he so rashly and diligently cut loose from their moorings.

Today the intelligent sons and daughters of the old-time European freebooters, despoilers, and imperial pirates tremble with moral consternation at what their forefathers did. Says Gunnar Myrdal, in his *An International Economy,* page 168 (Harper and Brothers: New York, 1956):

"The horrible vision often enters my mind of the ultimate results of our continuing and rapidly speeding up the practice, well established in some countries during the era of colonialism, of tossing together ever bigger crowds of illiterate proletarians— these new proletariats being even more uprooted than they were in the stagnant villages where they lived in the remnants of some culture and some established mores."

Who *took* here? Who *gave?* It is too complicated a process to admit of such simple questions. But the Europeans naively called it soul-saving, money-making, modern administration, missions of civilization, *Pax Britannica,* and a host of other equally quaint appellations. History is a strange story. Men enact history with one set of motives and the consequences that flow from such motivated actions often have nothing whatsoever to do with such motives. What irony will history reveal when those pages of Europe's domination of Asia and Africa are finally and honestly written! That history will depict a ghastly racial tragedy; it will expose a blind spot on the part of white Westerners that will make those who read that history laugh with a sob in their throats. The white Western world, until relatively recently the most secular and free part of the earth—with a secularity and freedom that was the secret of its power (science and industry)— labored unconsciously and tenaciously for five hundred years to make Asia and Africa (that is, the elite in those areas) more secular-minded than the West!

In the minds of hundreds of millions of Asians and Africans the traditions of their lives have been psychologically condemned beyond recall. Hundreds of millions live uneasily with beliefs of which they have been made ashamed. I say, *"Bravo!"* for that clumsy and cruel deed. Not to the motives, mind you, behind those deeds, motives which were all too often ignoble and base. But I do say "Bravo!" to all the consequences of Western plundering, a plundering that created the conditions for the possible rise of rational societies for the greater majority of mankind.

But enough of ironic comparisons. Where do we stand today? That part of the heritage of the West that I value—man stripped of the past and free for the future—has now been established as lonely bridgeheads in Asia and Africa in the form of a Western-educated elite, an elite that is more Western, in most cases, than the West. Tragic and lonely and all too often misunderstood are these men of the Asian-African elite. The West hates and fears that elite, and I must, to be honest, say that the instincts of the West that prompt that hate and fear are, on the whole, correct. For this elite in Asia and Africa constitutes islands of free men, the FREEST MEN IN ALL THE WORLD TODAY. They stand poised, nervous, straining at the leash, ready to go, with no weight of the dead past clouding their minds, no fears of foolish customs benumbing their consciousness, eager to build industrial civilizations. What does this mean? It means that the spirit of the Enlightenment, of the Reformation, which made Europe great, now has a chance to be extended to all mankind! A part of the non-West is now akin to a part of the West. East and West have become compounded. The partial overcoming of the forces of tradition and oppressive religions in Europe resulted, in a roundabout manner, in a partial overcoming of tradition and religion in decisive parts of Asia and Africa. The unspoken assumption in this history has been: WHAT IS GOOD FOR EUROPE IS GOOD FOR ALL MANKIND! I say: So be it.

I approve of what has happened. My only regret is that Europe could not have done what she did in a deliberate and intentional manner, could not have planned it as a global project. My wholehearted admiration would have gone out to the spirit of a Europe that had had the imagination to have launched this mighty revolution out of the generosity of its heart, out of a sense of lofty responsibility. Europe could then stand proudly before all the world and say: "Look at what we accomplished! We remade man in our image! Look at the new form of life that we brought into being!" And I'm sure that had that happened, the majority of mankind would have been Western in a sense that no atoms or hydrogen bombs can make a man Western. But, alas, that chance, that rare and noble opportunity, is gone forever. Europe missed the boat.

How can the spirit of the Enlightenment and the Reformation be extended now to all men? How can this accidental boon be made global in effect? That is the task that history now imposes upon us. Can a way be found, purged of racism and profits, to melt the rational areas and rational personnel of Europe with those of Asia and Africa? How can the curtains of race, color, religion, and tradition—all of which hamper man's mastery of his environment—be collectively rolled back by free men of the West and non-West? Is this a Utopian dream? Is this mere wishing? No. It is more drastic than that. The nations of Asia and Africa and Europe contain too much of the forces of the irrational for anyone to think that the future will take care of itself. The islands of the rational in the East are too tenuously held to permit of optimism. And the same is true of Europe. (We have but to recall reading of ideas to "burn up entire continents" to doff our illusions.) The truth is that our world—a world for all men, black, brown, yellow, and white—will either be all rational or totally irrational. For better or worse, it will eventually be one world.

How can these rational regions of the world be maintained? How can the pragmatically useful be made triumphant? Does this entail a surrender of the hard-bought national freedoms on the part of non-Western nations? I'm convinced that that will not happen, for these Asian and African nations, led by Western-educated leaders, love their freedom as much as the West loves its own. They have had to struggle and die for their freedom and they value it passionately. It is unthinkable that they, so recently freed from color and class domination of the West, would voluntarily surrender their sovereignty. Let me state the problem upside down. What Western nation would dream of abdicating its sovereignty and collaborating with powers that once so recently ruled them in the name of interests that were not their own—powers that created a vast literature of hate against them? Such an act would be irrational in the extreme. And the Western-educated leaders of non-Western nations are filled with too much distrust of an imperial-minded West to permit of any voluntary relinquishing of their control over their destinies.

Is there no alternative? *Must* there be a victorious East or a victorious West? If one or the other must win completely, then the fragile values won so blindly and accidentally and at so great a cost and sacrifice will be lost for us all. Where is the crux of this matter? Who is to act first? Who *should* act first? The burden of action rests, I say, with the West. For it was the West, however naively, that launched this vast historical process of the transformation of mankind. And of what must the action of the West consist? The West must aid and, yes, abet the delicate and tragic elite in Asia and Africa to establish rational areas of living. THE WEST, IN ORDER TO KEEP BEING WESTERN, FREE, AND SOMEWHAT RATIONAL, MUST BE PREPARED TO ACCORD TO THE ELITE OF ASIA AND AFRICA A FREEDOM WHICH IT ITSELF NEVER PERMITTED IN ITS OWN DOMAIN. THE ASIAN AND AFRICAN ELITE MUST BE GIVEN ITS HEAD! The West must perform an act of faith and do this. Such a mode of action has long been implied in the very nature of the ideas which the West has instilled into that Asian-African elite. The West must trust that part of itself that it has thrust, however blunderingly, into Asia and Africa. Nkrumah, Nasser, Sukarno, and Nehru, and the Western-educated heads of these newly created national states, must be given *carte blanche* to modernize their lands without overlordship of the West, and we must understand the methods that they will feel compelled to use.

Never, you will say. That is impossible, you will declare. Oh, I'm asking a hard thing and I know it. I'm Western, remember, and I know how horribly implausible my words sound to Westerners so used to issuing orders and having those orders obeyed at gun point. But what rational recourse does the West possess other than this? None.

If the West cannot do this, it means that the West does not believe in itself, does not trust the ideas which it has cast into the world. Yes, Sukarno, Nehru, Nasser, and others will necessarily use quasi-dictatorial methods to hasten the process of social evolution and to establish order in their lands—lands which were left spiritual voids by a too-long Western occupation and domination. Why pretend to be shocked at this? You would do the same if you were in their place. You have done it in the West over and over again. You do it in every war you fight, in every crisis, political or economic, you have. And don't you feel and know that, as soon as order has been established by your Western-educated leaders, they will, in order to be powerful, surrender the personal power that they have had to wield?*

Let us recognize what our common problem really is. Let us rethink what the issue is. This problem is vast and complicated. Merely to grasp it takes an act of the imagination. This problem, though it has racial overtones, is not racial. Though it has religious aspects, it is not religious. Though it has strong economic motives, it is not wholly economic. And though political action will, no doubt, constitute the main means, the *modus operandi,* of its solution, the problem is not basically political.

The problem is freedom. How can Asians and Africans be free of their stultifying traditions and customs and become industrialized, and powerful, if you like, like the West?

I say that the West cannot ask the elite of Asia and Africa, even though educated in the West, to copy or ape what has happened in the West. Why? Because the West has never really been honest with itself about how it overcame its own traditions and blinding customs.

Let us look at some examples of Western interpretation of its own history. A Civil War was fought in America and American school children are taught that it was to free the black slaves. It was not. It was to establish a republic, to create conditions of economic freedom, to clear the ground for the launching of an industrial society. (Naturally, slavery had to go in such a situation. I'm emphasizing the positive historic aspects, not the negative and inevitable ones!) The French fought a long and bloody Revolution and French school children are taught that it was for Liberty, Equality, and Fraternity. Yet we know that it was for the right of a middle class to think, to buy and sell, to enable men with talent to rise in their careers, and to push back (which was inevitable and implied) the power of the Church and the nobility.

*Here is a paradox: Nehru is as powerful as an emperor; Nkrumah is a *de facto* dictator; yet both men are staunch democrats and are using their vast personal power to sponsor measures that will undermine their "cult of the personality"! The key to their motives is that they seek power not for themselves, but for their people!

The English, being more unintentionally forthright than others, never made much bones about the fact that the freedom that they fought for was a freedom of trade.

Do these misinterpretations of Western history by the West negate the power and net historical gains of the Western world? No. It is not what the West said it did, but what the results really were that count in the long run.

Why have I raised these points of Western contradictions? Because, when non-Westerners, having the advantage of seeing more clearly—being psychologically *outside* of the West—what the West did, and when non-Westerners seek to travel that same road, the West raises strong objections, moral ones. I've had a white Westerner tell me: "You know, we must stay in Africa to protect the naked black natives. If we leave, the blacks we have educated will practice fascism against their own people." So this man was in a position to endorse the shooting down of a black elite because that black elite wanted to impose conditions relating to the control of imports and exports, something which his country practiced every day with hordes of armed policemen to enforce the laws regulating imports and exports!

The same objections are leveled against Nkrumah in the Gold Coast, against Sukarno in Indonesia, against Nasser in Egypt, against Nehru in India. Wise Westerners would insist that stern measures be taken by the elite of Asia and Africa to overcome the irrational forces of racism, superstition, etc. But if a selfish West hamstrings the elite of Asia and Africa, distrusts their motives, a spirit of absolutism will rise in Asia and Africa and will provoke a spirit of counterabsolutism in the West. In case that happens, all will be lost. We shall all, Asia and Africa as well as Europe, be thrown back into an age of racial and religious wars, and the precious heritage—the freedom of speech, the secular state, the independent personality, the autonomy of science—which is not Western or Eastern, but human, will be snuffed out of the minds of men.

The problem is freedom from a dead past. And freedom to build a rational future. How much are we willing to risk for freedom? I say let us risk everything. Freedom begets freedom. Europe, I say to you before it is too late: Let the Africans and Asians whom you have educated in Europe have their freedom, or you will lose your own in trying to keep freedom from them.

But how can this be done? Have we any recent precedent for such procedure? Is my suggestion outlandish? Unheard of? No. A ready answer and a vivid example are close at hand. A scant ten years ago we concluded a tragically desperate and costly war in Europe to beat back the engulfing tides of an irrational fascism. During those tense and eventful days I recall hearing Winston Churchill make this appeal to the Americans, when Britain was hard-pressed by hordes of German and Italian fascists:

"Give us the tools and we'll finish the job."

Today I say to the white men of Europe:

"You have, however misguidedly, trained and educated an elite in Africa and Asia. You have implanted in their hearts the hunger for freedom and rationality. Now this elite of yours—your children, one might say—is hard-pressed by hunger, disease, poverty, by stagnant economic conditions, by unbalanced class structures of their societies, by surging tides of racial shame, by oppressive and irrational tribal religions. You men of Europe made an abortive beginning to solve that problem. You failed. Now, I say to you: Men of Europe, give that elite the tools and let it finish that job!"

FREEDOM IS INDIVISIBLE.

3

The Literature of the Negro in the United States

To most people the literature of the American Negro is fairly well-known. So for me to give you merely a bare, bald recital of what Negroes have written would, in my opinion, be shirking a duty and a responsibility. Indeed, it would be the easy and the lazy way out, and I don't like the easy and lazy ways out of things.

As we all know, anthologists are legion today; to make an anthology requires simply this: Get a big pile of books on a given subject together, a big pot of glue, and a pair of sharp scissors and start clipping and pasting.

I do most seriously want to tell you about Negro writing, but I also want to try to tell you what some of that writing means, how it came to be written, what relationship it had to its time, and what it means to us today. In short, I'd like to try to interpret some of it for you; but one cannot interpret without thinking, without comparing. And, for the most part, I'm going to use Negro poets and their poems as my examples; for poets and poems have a way of telling a lot in a compressed manner.

But, first, I'm going to try to deposit certain concepts in your mind about the world in which we live; then, using these concepts as a magnifying glass, we will look at some of the literary utterances of the American Negro. The concepts I shall deal with are familiar, though I doubt if they've been applied to American Negro expression before. Let me start by making a general comparison.

A few years ago I spent some months living in the heart of French Quebec, on an island in the St. Lawrence River, about fifteen miles from the city of Quebec. As you no doubt know, the Province of Quebec represents one of the few real surviving remnants of feudal culture on the American continent. It has a Catholic culture, a close, organic, intimate, mainly rural, way of life. For more than three hundred years, many of the customs and habits of life of French Canadians have not changed.

Never before had I the experience of living intimately in a culture so different from the Protestant, Puritan culture of my own native land. And, like most travelers, I saw French Canadian culture with two pairs of eyes: I saw the Catholic culture of French Quebec, and, at the same time, I saw how different that culture was from the culture of industrial, Protestant America.

Now you may feel that I'm going rather far astray in talking about Negro literature by describing a culture in which there are practically no Negroes, but I have my reasons for this.

In French Quebec the Catholic church dominates all personal and institutional and political phases of life from the cradle to the grave. There is no split between the personal and the political; they are one. In telling you these facts, please understand I'm making no judgment upon the culture of French Quebec. I'm merely trying to present a few facts for the purpose of establishing a basis of comparison. The people of French Quebec are at one with their culture; they express themselves in and through it. The personalities of the people I met were serene, even-tempered; no one strove too hard for a personal or an individualistic vision of life. No one sought a separate or unique destiny; they were not a romantic people. The secular and the sacred are united in French Quebec; the social and the personal are integrated; the individual and his group are one.

How different this is from our culture! In America we are split up in almost every imaginable way. We have no central unity; our church and state are separate. With but a tiny area of agreement, each individual lives in his own world.

This break with the past was accomplished when we broke with the feudal world, and we call this Freedom, and it is the crowning development of the industrial West; it has given us the most powerful civilization the world has ever known. But, also, it has given us millions of wrecked lives, millions of oppressed. It has given us anti-Semitism, anti-Negroism. It has given us spectacular crime, corruption, violence, and a singular disregard for the individual. Yet I feel that we were right in breaking with the feudal world. We do not have and we do not need an official creed to which all must bow. Yet we have an industrial civilization that breeds restlessness, eagerness, an almost neurotic anxiety that there is a hidden meaning that each must wring from life before he dies lest he feel that he has failed.

How does this relate to the Negro in America? In this way: The Negro, like everybody else in America, came originally from a simple, organic way of life, such as I saw in French Quebec. And you must remember that your forefathers also came from the feudal cultures of Europe. It was from the total, oppressive cultures like those of French Quebec that men fled three centuries ago to settle in the New World. You are now adjusted to industrial life and perhaps you have forgotten that your forefathers once endured the agony of leaving their homes and native lands to settle in America. So, in historical outline, the lives of American Negroes closely resemble your own.

There are, of course, some few important differences; most whites left Europe voluntarily; the American Negro was snatched by force from the organic, warm, tribal culture of Africa, transported across the Atlantic in crowded, stinking ships, and sold into slavery. Held in bondage, stripped of his culture, denied family life for centuries, made to labor for others, the Negro tried to learn to live the life of the New World in an atmosphere of rejection and hate.

You see now why I feel that one ought to use the same concepts in discussing Negro life that one uses in discussing white life? It is the same life lifted to the heights of pain and pathos, drama and tragedy. The history of the Negro in America is the history of America written in vivid and bloody terms; it is the history of Western Man writ small. It is the history of men who tried to adjust themselves to a world whose laws, customs, and instruments of force were leveled against them. The Negro is America's metaphor.

Let me sum up the meaning of my comparison, for what it means will form the foundation of what I'll have to say to you about Negro literature. Let us imagine an abstract line and at one end of this line let us imagine a simple, organic culture—call it Catholic, feudal, religious, tribal, or what you will. Here are some of the features of that culture: It is bigger than the individual and the individual finds his meaning for living in it. The individual does not help to make up the rules or laws of that culture.

At the opposite end of our imaginary line, let us imagine another culture, such as the one in which we live. In contrast to entity, in which the personality is swallowed up, we have a constant striving for identity. Instead of preindividualism, we have a strident individualism. Whereas French Quebec has holy days, we have holidays. Church bells toll the time of day in French Quebec; we look at our watches to see the hour. Fetes become festivals.

The distance between these two cultures is the distance between feudal Europe and present-day, vibrant, nervous, industrial America. And it is the distance between the tribal African culture of the Negro and the place which he now occupies, against such great and constant odds, in American life.

It will be along this imaginary line—between these two culture types—that I'll string the Negro writers I'll discuss. For the development of Negro expression—as well as the whole of Negro life in America—hovers always somewhere between the rise of man from his ancient, rural way of life to the complex, industrial life of our time. Let me sum up these differences by contrast; entity vs. identity; preindividualism vs. individualism; the determined vs. the free.

Now, with this idea in mind, let me read you a short passage from the work of a world-famous Negro writer, a writer whose identity I shall withhold from you for a moment:

> "Sire, I am sorry to tell your majesty a cruel fact; but the feeling in Dauphiné is far from resembling that of Provence. The mountaineers are all Bonapartists, Sire."
>
> "Then," murmured Louis XVIII, "he was well informed. And how many men had he with him?"
>
> "I do not know, Sire," answered the minister of police.
>
> "What! You do not know? Have you neglected to obtain information of this circumstance? It is true this is of small importance," the king added with a withering smile.
>
> "Sire, it was impossible to learn; the dispatch simply stated the fact of the landing and the route taken by the traitor."
>
> "And how did this dispatch reach you?" inquired the king.
>
> The minister bowed his head, and while a deep color overspread his cheeks, he stammered, "By the telegraph, Sire."
>
> Louis XVIII advanced a step, folded his arms over his chest as Napoleon would have done. "So, then," he exclaimed, turning pale with anger, "seven allied armies overthrew that man. A miracle of Heaven replaced me on the throne after twenty-five years in exile . . ."

Did a Negro write that? It does not sound Negroid. And were Negroes ever in this world so intimately associated with any culture that they could write of kings and ministers and battles involving Louis XVIII?

Well, what I just quoted to you was a short passage from Alexander Dumas' *The Count of Monte Cristo*. Yes, it's true that Dumas was a Negro according to American racial codes, but his being a Negro was the least important thing about him. Why? Because there were no laws or customs barring him from the society in which he lived. He could attend any school he wanted to; he could go to any church he wanted to; he could engage in any profession he wanted to; he could live where he wanted to; he could marry whom he wanted to; and if he had the mind and talent, he could win fame if he wanted to. He did win fame. He was at one with the culture in which he lived, and he wrote out of the commonly shared hopes and expectations of his age.

Let me recall to you the imaginary, entity culture that we placed at one end of our line: a religious, tribal, feudal culture, a culture like that of French Quebec. I don't mean that a culture of this sort is an ideal for which we must strive; I put that culture at the end of an imaginary line to serve us as a guide, as a yardstick against which we could measure how well or ill men adjusted themselves.

We can say that Dumas was integrated with the culture of France and was a Frenchman.

Let me read you yet another passage from another Negro writer, a world famous one too:

The dawn was breaking. I was standing at my appointed place with my three seconds. With inexplicable impatience I awaited my opportunity. The spring sun rose, and it was already growing hot. I saw my opponent coming on foot, accompanied by just one second. We advanced to meet him. He approached holding his cap filled with cherries. The seconds measured twelve paces for us. I had to fire first, but my agitation was so great, that I could not depend upon the steadiness of my hands; and in order to give myself time to become calm, I ceded to my opponent the first shot. My adversary would not agree to this. It was decided that we should cast lots. The first number fell to him. He took aim and his bullet went through my cap. . . .

Is this Negro writing? It does not sound like the expressions of Negroes who live in America today. Did Negroes ever engage in duels? Well, what I have just read to you is a passage from a short story by Alexander Pushkin, a Russian Negro who was more a Russian than a Negro. Like Alexander Dumas, he had no cause to lament that he was a Negro; his writing does not carry any of the bitter and wild echoes of hate, frustration, and revolt found in the writings of American Negroes. Pushkin wrote out of the rich tradition of Russian realism, and he helped to further and enrich that tradition. He was one with his culture; he went to the schools of his choice; he served in an army that was not Jim Crow; he worked where he wanted to; he lived where he wanted to; and there was no sense of psychological distance between him and the culture of the land in which he lived.

Let me recall to you once again the concept we started with: Entity, men Integrated with their culture; and identity, men who are at odds with their culture, striving for personal identification. The writings I've just read to you were the work of men who were emotionally integrated with their country's culture; no matter what the color of their skins, they were not really Negroes. One was a Russian, the other was a Frenchman.

Has any American Negro ever written like Dumas or Pushkin? Yes, one. Only one. As though in irony, history decided that the first Negro who was to express himself with any degree of competence on the soil of America should strike a universal note. Before the webs of slavery had so tightened as to snare nearly all Negroes in our land, one was freed by accident to give utterance in poetry to what she felt, to give in clear, bell-like, limpid cadences the hope of freedom in the New World.

One day, in 1761, a slave ship, having made the horrible voyage from Africa to America, dropped anchor in Boston harbor. As usual an auction was held, with the slaves stripped naked and made to stand in public upon blocks. Would-be purchasers probed their fingers about the bodies of the black men and women to determine if they were sound of limb. Finally, all the slaves, except a delicate twelve-year-old black girl, were sold. Because she seemed too frail to render a good day's hard work, no one wanted her. But a Boston tailor by the name of Wheatley bought her and took her home, where she was trained to be the personal servant of Mrs. Wheatley.

This nameless black child was given the name of Phyllis and was accepted into the Wheatley home as one of the family, enjoying all the rights of the other Wheatley children. She displayed a remarkable talent for learning and she was taught to read and write. Need I point out that this African-born child possessed dim recollections of her mother pouring out water to the rising sun, no doubt a recollection of some kind of tribal, African ceremony? Slavery had not yet cast its black shadow completely over the American scene, and the minds of white people were not so warped at that time as they are now regarding the capacities of the Negro. Hence, the Wheatley family was quite free of inhibitions about educating Phyllis; they proceeded to educate her in the so-called classical manner; that is, she got the kind of education that the white girls of her time received.

At an early age she was writing verse, influenced by the heroic couplets of Pope, the reigning English poet of that time. Closely bound to the Wheatley family, absorbing the impulses of the Christian community in which she lived, sharing the culture of her country in terms of home and school and church, her poetry showed almost no traces of her being a Negro or having been born in Africa. Indeed, so closely integrated was she with the passions and hopes of America that, in the War of 1776, she wrote a poem about George Washington. She was received by Washington at his military headquarters and the Father of Our Country complimented her upon her poetic utterances. In praise of Washington and in rebuke to imperialistic England, Phyllis Wheatley wrote:

> *Ah! cruel blindness to Columbia's state!*
> *Lament thy thirst of boundless power too late.*

Proceed great chief, with virtue on thy side,
Thy ev'ry action let the goddess guide.
A crown, a mansion, and a throne that shine,
With gold unfading, Washington, be thine.

There is a note of irony embedded in the life of this girl who wrote revolutionary poetry though her skin was black and she was born in Africa; she made a trip to England where the Countess of Huntingdon wanted to present her to the Court of George III, and only ill health robbed her of that honor. (This was, of course, after the Revolutionary War.)

Again let me recall to you the concept I mentioned before. Phyllis Wheatley was at one with her culture. What a far cry this is from the Negro Seabees who staged a sit-down strike a few years ago on the Pacific Coast when the war against Japan was at its hardest! What makes for this difference in loyalty? Are the three excerpts I've read to you the writing of Negroes? No, not by present-day American standards. Then, what is a Negro? What is Negro writing?

Being a Negro has to do with the American scene, with race hate, rejection, ignorance, segregation, discrimination, slavery, murder, fiery crosses, and fear. But we will examine that when we come to it.

At last we have found on the American scene, in the writing of Phyllis Wheatley, someone whom we can establish at the head of our imaginary line. Now we can use her as a guide, a yardstick to measure the degree of integration of other Negro writers.

Suppose the personalities of many Phyllis Wheatleys of America had been allowed to develop? What a different nation we might have been! What a different literary utterance the American Negro might have given voice to! But, as we move on to other Negro literary figures, a queer spell at once comes over the scene. We cannot examine other Negro literary figures without taking into account something terrible that was happening to Negroes in the United States.

Even though we had won the War of Independence, there was

a reaction against the ideals of Patrick Henry and Thomas Jefferson; the cotton gin was invented and vast new lands were opened up in the South. Slavery grew from a tentative gesture into the greatest single aggregate of political power in the nation. There followed decades of killings and burnings and lynchings and beatings and futile hope on the part of the Negroes. Stripped of his tribal African culture and not allowed to partake of the culture of the New World, the Negro was consistently brutalized, reduced to a creature of impulse who worked in the fields. Again and again he tried to revolt, hurling himself against his foes who outnumbered him, but in vain. It was but natural then that the nature of Negro literary utterance would change.

The next Negro literary figure I want to call to your attention is that of George Moses Horton, born in 1797 and died in 1883. The dates of his birth and death are important, for they span the bloodiest period of the history of the Negro in America. Born in North Carolina, he was a slave of the Horton family; but his relationship to that family differed greatly from that of the Phyllis Wheatley relationship to the Boston family in which she was reared. Horton was passed around from one member of the Horton family to another; finally, in 1865, his master allowed him to hire himself out. While working around the home of a university president, he learned to read and write; for years he was a village character, regarded with amusement by the white students. He hired himself out as a writer of verse, charging twenty-five and fifty cents for a poetic job.

Finally some of his verse crept into print; not too much is known about this obscure wanderer's life, but we can guess at what he really felt from the following lines:

> Alas! and am I born for this,
> To wear this slavish chain?
> Deprived of all created bliss,
> Through hardship, toil and pain!
>
> . . . .

> *Oh, Heaven! and is there no relief*
> *This side the silent grave—*
> *To soothe the pain—to quell the grief*
> *And anguish of a slave?*

The poem runs on, lamenting, fighting, imploring. Something has happened since Phyllis Wheatley wrote. Entity has turned into a kind of sullen, raging sense of rebellious identity. Horton certainly was not at one with his culture, but neither had he completely broken away. He writes in English and tries to express himself in the poetic traditions of his time, but there is now a sense of psychological distance between him and the land in which he lives. Horton was an emotionally trapped man; he lived in a culture of which he was not really a part; he was a split man, believing and feeling something which he could not live; he was an agonizingly self-conscious man, always longing to perform an act against which there existed a dreadful taboo!

We are now, it seems, approaching the literature of the American Negro and I think that you can readily see what it is that makes the difference between American Negro writing and just plain American writing. Horton's writing does not stem from racial feeling, but from a social situation; and Horton's cry for freedom was destined to become the tradition of Negro literature in the United States. Almost unbrokenly this tradition of lament was to roll down the decades, swelling, augmenting itself, becoming a vast reservoir of bitterness and despair and infrequent hope. This tradition of bitterness was to become so complex, was to assume such a tight, organic form, that most white people would think, upon examining it, that all Negroes had embedded in their flesh and bones some peculiar propensity toward lamenting and complaining.

From now on we plunge into a welter of crude patterns of surging hate and rebellion; from Horton's time on but few Negroes would even possess the opportunity to live in stable family units.

Another Negro poet, James M. Whitfield, born in 1830 and died in 1870, was a barber by trade. Whitfield was born in Boston, then moved to Buffalo, New York; and not too much is known about how he came to write. His first poetic utterances were so favorably received that he quit barbering and took to the public platform; and his poems continue the tradition of Horton:

> America, it is to thee,
> Thou boasted land of liberty,—
> It is to thee that I raise my song,
> Thou land of blood, and crime, and wrong.
> It is to thee my native land,
> From which has issued many a band
> To tear the black man from his soil
> And force him here to delve and toil
> Chained on your blood-bemoistened sod,
> Cringing beneath a tyrant's rod . . .

As you see, the fact of separation from the culture of his native land has now sunk home into the Negro's heart; the Negro loves his land, but that land rejects him. Here we can witness the slow emergence of a new type of personality; here is the beginning of insecurity as a way of life; of violence as a daily companion.

The next Negro poet to attract attention in America was a woman, Frances Ellen Harper; living from 1825 to 1911, her life spanned slavery, war, emancipation, and freedom; and when she put her pen to paper her eyes were filled with more scenes of violence than perhaps many of our soldiers saw in the war just ended. In a poem entitled "Bury Me in a Free Land," she says:

> Make me a grave where'er you will
>   In a lowly plain, or a lofty hill;
> Make it among the earth's humblest graves,
>   But not in a land where men are slaves.
> I could not rest if around my grave
>   I heard the steps of a trembling slave;

> *His shadow above my silent tomb*
> *Would make it a place of fearful gloom.*

Truly, you must now know that the word Negro in America means something not racial or biological, but something purely social, something made in the United States. Poems such as the above seem to imply that the eyes of the American Negro were fastened in horror upon something from which he could not turn away. The Negro could not take his eyes off the auction block: he never had a chance to; he could not stop thinking of lynching: he never had a chance to. The Negro writer had no choice in his subject matter; he could not select his experiences. Hence, the monotonous repetition of horror that rolls in verse from one generation to another.

Let us pursue this melancholy tale.

Albery A. Whitman, born 1851 and died 1902, spanning with his life slavery, war, freedom, also spoke a tongue that denied him, belonged to a culture that rejected him, walked upon a soil that mocked him, and lived and labored among men who hated him.

In his poem "The Rape of Florida," he says:

> *So fared the land where slaves were groaning yet—*
> *Where beauty's eyes must feed the lusts of men!*
> *'Tis as when horrid dreams we half forget,*
> *Would then relate, and still relate again—*
> *Ah! Cold abhorrence hesitates my pen!*
> *The heavens were sad, and hearts of men were faint;*
> *Philanthropy implored and wept, but then*
> *The Wrong, unblushing trampled on Restraint,*
> *While feeble Law sat by and uttered no complaint.*

In the verse of Whitman we see the beginnings of complexity; he too wrote of wrong, but there was in his rhymes a desire to please. But the split in Negro personality deepened despite the fact that men like Whitman strove to weave color and drama and movement into their poems. A tradition of bitterness has set in; the basic theme is now set, and there is no escape from it. All black lips that now sing pay tribute to the power of oppression. It is true that there was an urge in some black singers to write so that the whites would buy their poems; but in them no less than in others this sense of distance could not be ignored. So, self-consciously, while hiding what they saw and knew to be true, knew to be the real meaning of their lives, some Negro poets deliberately put forth the lighter, the more lyrical, side for *white* consumption.

The most gifted, vivid, and popular black poet to pay tribute to this contradiction was Paul Laurence Dunbar. During his tragically brief career (1872–1906), no sweeter verse than his was written in America:

> *Ere sleep comes down to soothe the weary eyes,*
> *Which all the day with ceaseless care have sought*
> *The magic gold which from the seeker flies;*
> *Ere dreams put on the gown and cap of thought,*
> *And make the waking world of lies—*
> *Of lies most palpable, uncouth, forlorn,*
> *That say life's full of aches and tears and sighs,—*
> *Oh, how with more than dreams the soul is torn,*
> *Ere sleep comes down to soothe the weary eyes.*

Dunbar was the first Negro singer to be really helped by whites; he was fostered by William Dean Howells and his verse was published in the leading periodicals of his time. He labored hard to fill the many commissions that poured in upon him; but through his lyrical songs now and again there broke a sense of the paradox that was his life, as in the following poem:

> *I know why the caged bird sings, ah me,*
> *When his wing is bruised and his bosom sore,—*
> *When he beats his bars and would be free;*
> *It is not a carol of joy or glee,*

> But a prayer that he sends from his heart's deep core,
> But a plea, that upward to Heaven he flings—
> I know why the caged bird sings!

Then there were times when he spoke out what was in his heart:

> We smile, but, Oh great Christ, our cries
> To thee from tortured souls arise.
> We sing, but oh the clay is vile
> Beneath our feet, and long the mile;
> But let the world dream otherwise,
>   We wear the mask.

Dunbar wrote many novels and poems which had wide sales. But there was a fatal conflict in him; he drank heavily to drown it, to resolve it, and failed. He tells us but little of what he really felt, but we know that he tried to turn his eyes as much as possible from that vision of horror that had claimed the exclusive attention of so many Negro writers, tried to communicate with his country as a man. Perhaps no other Negro writer ever demanded more of himself than Dunbar did, and that he achieved so much, that he did manage to wring a little unity out of the blatant contradiction that was his life, is truly remarkable.

The black singers who followed Dunbar, however, cared less about what their *white* friends thought and more about what *they* felt, and they resumed the tradition, sensing that the greatest and deepest meaning of their lives lay in it, that all that was truly human in them had to be wrung from its dark and painful depths.

But let us catch up with ourselves. Expression springs out of an environment, and events modify what is written by molding consciousness. From 1761 to 1900, roughly speaking, a kind of unity knit Negro expression together. But, starting with emancipation, many kinds of stratification took place in Negro life; Negroes became separated from Negroes, the rich from the poor, the ignorant from the educated, the city Negro from the country Negro, and so on.

While this stratification was taking place among Negroes, white attitudes gradually hardened and a still further atomization of Negro life took place, creating personality types far below even those that existed in slavery. Around the turn of the century, two tendencies became evident in Negro expression. I'll call the first tendency: The Narcissistic Level, and the second tendency I'll call: The Forms of Things Unknown, which consists of folk utterances, spirituals, blues, work songs, and folklore.

These two main streams of Negro expression—The Narcissistic Level and The Forms of Things Unknown—remained almost distinctly apart until the depression struck our country in 1929, when once again there surged up a tendency toward unity in Negro thought and feeling, though the traditional sense of distance still prevailed. This division in Negro life can be described in psychological as well as in class terms. It can be said there were Negroes who naively accepted what their lives were, lived more or less unthinkingly in their environment, mean as they found it, and sought escape either in religion, migration, alcohol, or in what I've called a sensualization of their sufferings in the form of jazz and blues and folk and work songs.

Then there were those who hoped and felt that they would ultimately be accepted in their native land as free men, and they put forth their claims in a language that their nation had given them. These latter were more or less always middle class in their ideology. But it was among the migratory Negro workers that one found, rejected and ignorant though they were, strangely positive manifestations of expression, original contributions in terms of form and content.

Middle-class Negroes borrowed the forms of the culture which they strove to make their own, but the migratory Negro worker improvised his cultural forms and filled those forms with a content wrung from a bleak and barren environment, an environment that stung, crushed, all but killed him.

But, before I tell of these migratory voices, let me explain what I mean by the Narcissistic Level of expression that prevailed among middle-class Negro writers, say, from 1900 to 1925.

Remember Phyllis Wheatley and how she was at one with her country? After her time that oneness was no longer possible with Negroes; race hate and Jim Crowism would not let them feel it.

But there were some few Negroes who, through luck, diligence, and courage, did rise and make the culture of their nation their own even though that nation still rejected them; and, having made the culture of their nation their own, they hurled pleading words against the deaf ears of white America until the very meaning of their lives came to be in telling how and what the rejection which their country leveled against them made them feel. You remember the Greek legend of Narcissus who was condemned by Nemesis to fall in love with his own reflection which he saw in the water of a fountain? Well, the middle-class Negro writers were condemned by America to stand before a Chinese Wall and wail that they were like other men, that they felt as others felt. It is this relatively static stance of emotion that I call The Narcissistic Level. These Negroes were in every respect the equal of whites; they were valid examples of personality types of Western culture; but they lived in a land where even insane white people were counted above them. They were men whom constant rejection had rendered impacted of feeling, choked of emotion. During the first quarter of this century, these men, Trotter, Du Bois, Washington, etc., fought as the Negro had never fought before for equal rights, but they fought in vain. It is true that when their voices reached the ears of many philanthropic whites, they did win a few concessions which helped Negro institutions to exist. But the irony in the efforts of these Negroes was that the gains they won fastened ever tighter around their necks the shackles of Jim Crowism. For example, every new hospital, clinic, and school that was built was a *Negro* hospital, a *Negro* clinic, a *Negro* school! So, though Negroes were slowly rising out of their debased physical conditions, the black ghettos were growing ever larger; instead of racial segregation lessening, it grew, deepened, spread. Today, Jim Crow institutions have fastened themselves organically upon the free soil of the nation and the Black Belt is commonplace.

While this was happening in the upper levels of Negro life, a chronic and grinding poverty set in in the lower depths. Semi-literate black men and women drifted from city to city, ever seeking what was not to be found: jobs, homes, love—a chance to live as free men. . . . Millions swarmed from the plantations to the small towns and cities of the South; and then from the southern towns and cities they flooded the northern industrial centers. Bereft of family life, poverty-stricken, bewildered, they moved restlessly amidst the highest industrial civilization the world has ever known, in it but not of it, unable to respond to the vivid symbols of power of an alien culture that met their eyes at every turn.

Because I feel personally identified with the migrant Negro, his folk songs, his ditties, his wild tales of bad men; and because my own life was forged in the depths in which they live, I'll tell first of the Forms of Things Unknown. Numerically, this formless folk utterance accounts for the great majority of the Negro people in the United States, and it is my conviction that the subject matter of future novels and poems resides in the lives of these nameless millions. There are two pools of this black folk expression: The sacred and the secular. (Let me recall to you quickly that we are now far beyond the world of Phyllis Wheatley; she was an integrated individual, at one with her culture; we are now dealing with people who have lost their individuality, whose reactions are fiercely elemental, whose shattered lives are burdened by impulses they cannot master or control.) It is from the sacred songs of the plantation that we get the pathos of:

Sometimes I feel like a motherless child
Sometimes I feel like a motherless child
Sometimes I feel like a motherless child
A long ways from home . . .
A long ways from home . . .

And then there is the nostalgia for another world, an unappeasable longing to escape a painful life:

> *Swing low, sweet chariot,*
> *Coming for to carry me home . . .*

And here is a paradoxical note of triumphant defeat:

> *Steal away, steal away, steal away to Jesus,*
> *Steal away, steal away home,*
> *I ain't got long to stay here . . .*

And here is militancy disguised in religious imagery:

> *Joshua fit the battle of Jericho,*
> *Jericho, Jericho,*
> *Joshua fit the battle of Jericho,*
> *And the walls came tumbling down . . .*

And tender, timid despair:

> *Oh, they whipped him up the hill, up the hill, up the hill*
> *Oh, they whipped him up the hill, up the hill, up the hill*
> *Oh, they whipped him up the hill, and he never said a*
> *mumbling word,*
> *He just hung down his head, and he cried . . .*

Outright rebellion is couched in Biblical symbols; is it not plain that the Negro is a Negro even in his religion, that his consciousness of being a rejected American seeps into his worship, his prayers . . . ?

> *If I had-a my way,*
> *I'd tear this building down.*
> *Great God, then, if I had-a my way*
> *If I had-a my way, little children,*

If I had-a my way,
I'd tear this building down . . .

These authorless utterances sprang spontaneously from the lips of slaves and they remain the single most significant contribution of folk and religious songs to our national culture. It was through the door of religion that the American Negro first walked into the house of Western culture, and it was through religious symbols that he has given voice to his most poignant yearnings. And yet, instead of his songs being mystical or metaphysical, they are simply and directly wish fulfillments, projections of his longings to escape his chains and blows.

And even when the Negro turns from the sacred to the secular, he seems unable to escape the burdens and consciousness of his racial plight that determines all, making him feel that he is a Negro before he is a man. Recognition of wrong comes even in lilting ditties:

We raise the wheat,
They give us the corn;
We bake the bread,
They give us the crust;
We sift the meal,
They give us the husk;
We peel the meat,
They give us the skin;
And that's the way
We skin the pot,
They give us the liquor,
And they say that's good enough for nigger.

We get hints of probable dirty work of slaves against their masters in this humorous ditty which tells of a master who promised freedom to a slave, and it brought about an attempt on the part of the slave to hasten his day of liberation:

Yes, my old master promise me;
But his papers didn't leave me free.
A dose of poison helped him along.
May the Devil preach his funeral song.

Even at the very bottom of Negro life there existed a knowledge of the dual existence they were forced to live; in this work song, a laborer states the problem:

Me and my captain don't agree
But he don't know, 'cause he don't ask me
He don't know, he don't know my mind
When he sees me laughing
Laughing to keep from crying
Got one mind for white folks to see
Another for what I know is me . . .

The impulses that prodded so many millions of southern Negroes to leave the plantations for the cities of the South, and the dissatisfaction that drove so many other millions from the cities of the South to the industrial centers of the North are summed up in the "Backwater Blues" as sung by Bessie Smith:

Then I went an' stood up on some high ol' lonesome hill
I went an' stood up on some high ol' lonesome hill
An' looked down on the house where I used to live

Backwater blues done cause me to pack mah things and go
Backwater blues done cause me to pack mah things and go
Cause mah house fell down an' I cain' live there no mo'

Many of them knew that their hope was hopeless, and it was out of this that the blues was born, the apex of sensual despair. A strange and emotional joy is found in contemplating the blackest aspects of life:

> *I'm going down to the river, set down on the ground*
> *I'm going down to the river, set down on the ground*
> *If the blues overtake me, I'll jump overboard and drown*

And what the psychoanalysts call ambivalence is put forward by illiterate Negroes in terms that would have shocked Dr. Freud:

> *I'm going to buy me a shotgun long as I am tall*
> *I'm going to buy me a shotgun just as long as I am tall*
> *I'm going to shoot my woman just to see her fall . . .*

In "Dink's Blues" we hear a death-wish vented against white people:

> *I wish to God that east-bound train would wreck*
> *I wish to God that east-bound train would wreck*
> *Kill the engineer, break the fireman's neck . . .*

Lower-class Negroes cannot be accused of possessing repressions or inhibitions! Out of the folk songs of the migrant Negro there has come one form of Negro folklore that makes even Negroes blush a little among themselves when it is mentioned. These songs, sung by more adult Negroes than would willingly admit it, sum up the mood of despairing rebellion. They are called *The Dirty Dozens.* Their origin is obscure but their intent is plain and unmistakable. They jeer at life; they leer at what is decent, holy, just, wise, straight, right, and uplifting. I think that it is because, from the Negro's point of view, it is the right, the holy, the just, that crush him in America. I'm sure that we've reached that point in our public life where straight, documentary facts can be presented without someone saying that they are in bad taste. I insist upon presenting *The Dirty Dozens* because they possess a meaning far beyond that of the merely risqué.

But first, picture to yourselves a vast mass of semi-literate people living amidst the most complex, the most highly industrialized, nation on earth, and try to understand these contradictions:

The Negro's shattered families lived amidst the most stable families of the land; his broken speech was uttered in the same neighborhoods where white people spoke flawlessly. The Negro had but to turn his eyes from his unpainted wooden shack and he saw the painted homes of whites. Out of this organic contradiction, the Negro hurled his hardest words against the white world in which he lived. He had no family life; well, why worry about that? Was it not the family life of whites above him that was crushing him? These Negroes seemed to have said to themselves: "Well, if what is happening to me is right, then, dammit, anything is right."

The Dirty Dozens extol incest, celebrate homosexuality; even God's ability to create a rational world is naively but scornfully doubted, as in the following ditty:

> *God made Him an elephant*
> *And He made him stout*
> *But He wasn't satisfied*
> *'Til He made him a snout*
> *And He made his snout*
> *Just as long as a rail*
> *But He wasn't satisfied*
> *'Til He made him a tail*
> *He made his tail*
> *Just to fan the flies*
> *But He wasn't satisfied*
> *'Til He made him some eyes*
> *He made his eyes*
> *Just to look on the grass*
> *But He wasn't satisfied*
> *'Til He made his yes yes yes*
> *He made his yes yes yes*
> *But He didn't get it fixed*
> *But He wasn't satisfied*
> *'Til He made him six*
> *He made him six, Lord,*

> *And He made them well*
> *So you know by that*
> *That the elephant caught hell . . .*

This is not atheism; this is beyond atheism; these people do not walk and talk with God; they walk and talk about Him. The seduction of virgins is celebrated with amoral delight:

> *Why your little sister*
>   *Why she ask me to kiss her*
> *I told her to wait*
>   *'Til she got a little bigger*
> *When she got a little bigger*
>   *She said I could kiss her*
> *You know by that, boys,*
>   *That I didn't miss her*
> *Now she's a dirty mistreat*
>   *A robber and a cheat*
> *Slip her in the dozens*
>   *Her papa is her cousin*
> *And her mama do the Lordy Lord . . .*

That white men who claimed that they followed the precepts of Christ should have been guilty of so much cruelty forced some nameless black bard to utter:

> *Our Father, who art in heaven*
> *White man owe me 'leven, and pay me seven,*
> *Thy kingdom come, thy will be done*
> *And ef I hadn't tuck that, I wouldn't got none.*

Do you catch the echoes of Communism here? If you do, you are suffering from an auditory illusion; for that irreverent ditty was written long before Communism was conceived of, long before Karl Marx wrote *Das Kapital*. If there's any Communism in that verse, it is of a divine origin.

A Negro woman exults consciously and publicly in the disorganization of life which America forces her to live:

> *My floor is dirty and my house ain't never clean*
> *My floor is dirty and my house ain't never clean*
> *Ain't got no husband but I got a dozen married men . . .*

Still another woman's knowledge of the sexual prowess of all the men living in her neighborhood reveals a compulsive promiscuity which she unashamedly and lyrically advertises:

> *There's nineteen men livin' in mah neighborhood*
> *Nineteen men livin' in mah neighborhood*
> *Eighteen of them are fools, an' de other ain' no doggone good*

Well, what do you want? What can you expect from men and women who have been driven out of life?

But there are times when these torrid moods of meanness are lifted by gifted writers to the level of social and political direction, as in the bitter, fighting lyrics of Warren Cuney, who sums up what Jim Crowism in wartime means to Negroes:

> *Well, airplanes flying across the land and the sea*
> *Everybody's flying but a Negro like me*
> *Uncle Sam says your place is on the ground*
> *When I fly my airplanes I want no Negroes around*
> *The same thing for the navy when ships go to sea*
> *All they got is a mess-boy's job for me . . .*

But what was happening, so to speak, upstairs, when the Negro migrants were venting their spleen against the world? If you remember, we left the Negro middle-class writers standing before the Chinese Wall of America, narcissistically preoccupied with their feelings, saying, "If you prick me, I bleed; if you put fire to me, I burn; I am like you who exclude me. . . ." Perhaps the most graphic and lyrical of these men was W. E. B. Du Bois;

indeed, one might say that it was with him that the Negro complaint reached almost religious heights of expression. Du Bois prays to God in public:

> *Listen to us, Thy children: our faces dark with doubt are*
> *made a mockery in Thy sanctuary. With uplifted hands we*
> *front Thy heaven, O God, crying;*
> *We beseech Thee to hear us, good Lord!*

And then, vehemently, in Old Testament style:

> *Doth not this justice of hell stink in Thy nostrils, O God?*
> *How long shall the mounting flood of innocent blood roar in*
> *Thine ears and pound in our hearts for vengeance? Pile the pale*
> *frenzy of blood-crazed brutes who do such deeds high on Thine*
> *altar, Jehovah, and burn it in hell forever and forever.*
> *Forgive us, good Lord! we know not what we say!*

Moods such as these have suffused the many books of Du Bois, and where the mood is absent *per se*, we find it projected in terms of history, fiction, verse. Here we see the outright curse of the Negro migrant lifted to a hymn of bitterness; here we see the long, drawn-out moan of the blues turned into a phrase of lament; here we see the brutal cynicism of illiterate Negroes converted into irony; here we watch the jerky lines of *The Dirty Dozens* transmute themselves into the surging rhythms of free verse; here indeed we see Pushkin and Dumas turned into raging, livid demons! Poor Phyllis Wheatley would have burned to a cinder if such searing emotions had ever entered her frail body.

Following Du Bois, James Weldon Johnson lifted his voice; listen to Johnson, as conservative a Negro as ever lived in America; but his eyes were riveted upon this:

> *Quick! Chain him to that oak! It will resist*
> *The fire much longer than this slender pine.*

Now bring the fuel! Pile it 'round him! Wait!
Pile not so fast or high, or we shall lose
The agony and terror in his face.
And now the torch! Good fuel that! the flames
Already leap head-high. Ha! hear that shriek!
And there's another! wilder than the first.
Fetch water! Water! Pour a little on
The fire, lest it should burn too fast. Hold so!
Now let it slowly blaze again. See there!
He squirms! He groans! His eyes bulge wildly out,
Searching around in vain appeal for help!

Was it otherwise with other writers? No. You've seen the images of horror that a conservative like James Weldon Johnson evoked. Yet, I, coming from an entirely different social stratum, wove the same vision of horror into another pattern in a poem called "Between the World and Me":

And one morning while in the woods I suddenly stumbled upon
*   the thing,*
Stumbled upon it in a grassy clearing guarded by scaly oaks and
*   elms.*
And the sooty details of the scene rose, thrusting themselves
*   between the world and me . . .*

There was a design of white bones slumbering forgottenly upon
*   a cushion of gray ashes.*
There was a charred stump of a sapling pointing a blunt finger
*   accusingly at the sky.*
There were torn tree limbs, tiny veins of burnt leaves, and a
*   scorched coil of greasy hemp;*
A vacant shoe, an empty tie, a ripped shirt, a lonely hat, and a
*   pair of trousers stiff with black blood.*
And upon the trampled grass were buttons, dead matches, butt-
*   ends of cigars and cigarettes, peanut shells, a drained gin-*
*   flask, and a whore's lipstick;*

Scattered traces of tar, restless arrays of feathers, and the lingering smell of gasoline.

And through the morning air the sun poured yellow surprise into the eye sockets of a stony skull . . .

And while I stood there my mind was frozen with a cold pity for the life that was gone.

The ground gripped my feet and my heart was circled with icy walls of fear—

The sun died in the sky; a night wind muttered in the grass and fumbled with leaves in the trees; the woods poured forth the hungry yelping of hounds; the darkness screamed with thirsty voices; and the witnesses rose and lived:

The dry bones stirred, rattled, lifted, melting themselves into my bones.

The gray ashes formed flesh firm and black, entering into my flesh.

The gin-flask passed from mouth to mouth; cigars and cigarettes glowed, the whore smeared the lipstick red upon her lips.

And a thousand faces swirled around me, clamoring that my life be burned . . .

And then they had me, stripped me, battering my teeth into my throat till I swallowed my own blood.

My voice was drowned in the roar of their voices, and my black wet body slipped and rolled in their hands as they bound me to the sapling.

And my skin clung to the bubbling hot tar, falling from me in patches,

And the down and the quills of the white feathers sank into my raw flesh, and I moaned in my agony.

Then my blood was cooled mercifully, cooled by a baptism of gasoline.

And in a blaze of red I leaped to the sky as pain rose like water, boiling my limbs.

Panting, begging, I clutched childlike, clutched to the hot sides of death.

> *Now I am dry bones and my face a stony skull staring in yellow*
>   *surprise at the sun . . .*

Did ever in history a race of men have for so long a time the same horror before their eyes? I know that for short periods horrors like this have come to men, but they ended at last; I know that in war horror fills the minds of all, but even wars pass. The horrors that confront Negroes stay in peace and war, in winter and summer, night and day.

Futility now enters the heart of the urban Negro; from the teeming city of Chicago Fenton Johnson comes with his testimony:

> *I am tired of work; I am tired of building up somebody else's*
> *civilization.*
>   *Let us take a rest, M'Lissy Jane.*
>   *I will go down to the Last Chance Saloon, drink a gallon or*
> *two of gin, shoot a game or two of dice and sleep the rest of the*
> *night on one of Mike's barrels . . .*

Then again racial bitterness enters:

> *Throw the children into the river; civilization has given us*
> *too many. It is better to die than grow up and find out that you*
> *are colored.*
>   *Pluck the stars out of the heavens. The stars mark our destiny.*
> *The stars marked my destiny.*
>   *I am tired of civilization.*

And then Claude McKay reaches a white-hot pitch of passion with:

> *Your door is shut against my tightened face,*
> *And I am sharp as steel with discontent;*
> *But I possess the courage and the grace*
> *To bear my anger proudly and unbent.*

> *The pavement slabs burn loose beneath my feet,*
> *A chafing savage, down the decent street;*
> *A passion rends my vitals as I pass*
> *Where boldly shines your shuttered door of glass.*
> *Oh, I must search for wisdom every hour,*
> *Deep in my wrathful bosom sore and raw,*
> *And find in it the superhuman power*
> *To hold me to the letter of your law!*
> *Oh, I must keep my heart inviolate*
> *Against the potent poison of your hate!*

Remember that white faces were hovering in the minds of black men when they wrote those lines; this is their judgment upon you and your world. Are we not a long, long way from the innocence of Phyllis Wheatley? To say that Claude McKay is a rebel is to understate it; his rebellion is a way of life.

Even when Negro poets become sensually lyrical now, they cannot escape the horrible vision of their life in America, as we can see in these lines of Jean Toomer:

> *O Negro slaves, dark purple ripened plums,*
> *Squeezed, and bursting in the pine-wood air,*
> *Passing, before they strip the old tree bare*
> *One plum was saved for me, one seed becomes*
> *An everlasting song, a singing tree,*
> *Caroling softly souls of slavery*
> *What they were, and what they are to me,*
> *Caroling softly souls of slavery.*

Even at the apex of lyrical utterance, color and race form the core of meaning for Countee Cullen, as in "Heritage":

> *What is Africa to me:*
> *Copper sun or scarlet sea,*
> *Jungle star or jungle track,*
> *Strong bronzed men, or regal black*

> *Women from whose loins I sprang*
> *When the birds of Eden sang?*

The conflict between the human needs of the Negro and what is demanded of him by white America reaches a point that all but overwhelms the poet:

> *All day long and all night through,*
> *One thing only must I do:*
> *Quench my pride, and cool my blood,*
> *Lest I perish in the flood. . . .*

No less than a black clergyman, James D. Corrothers, likens the plight of the Negro to that of Christ:

> *To be a Negro in a day like this*
> *　Demands forgiveness. Bruised with blow on blow,*
> *Betrayed, like Him whose woe-dimmed eyes gave bliss*
> *　Still must one succor those who brought one low,*
> *To be a Negro in a day like this.*

George Leonard Allen again stresses the Biblical theme in an attempt to awaken compassion by reminding America that she acts like Pilate toward her darker brother:

> *Lord, 'twas not I that slew my guiltless brother*
> *　Without a cause, save that his skin was black!*
> *Not my fierce hate, but that of many another*
> *　Stole what man's puny strength cannot give back!*

In a bitter, masochistic mood of self-laceration a black poet, Frank Horne, tries to see his people and himself through white American eyes:

> *Little Black Boy*
> *Chased down the street—*

"Nigger, nigger, never die
Black face and shiny eye,
Nigger . . . nigger . . . nigger."

A mood of poignant nostalgia makes Arna Bontemps evoke:

The golden days are gone. Why do we wait
So long upon the marble steps, blood
Falling from our open wounds? and why
Do our black faces search the sky?

But despair is not the entire picture. Each new generation of
Negro writers lived in an environment that was almost the same
until World War I; but that war provided the first real break in
this continuity of hopelessness. Out of the restlessness left in the
wake of World War I, Soviet Russia rose and sent out her calls to
the oppressed. Until that time the American Negro had to depend
upon white Americans for a definition of his problem, of his position, had to accept the friendship of white liberals. For three centuries white America told the Negro that nowhere on earth would
he be as highly regarded as in America; and the Negro had to
fight and plead within the frame of reference of that charitable
advice. But suddenly that spell was broken forever. Alien ideologies gripped men's minds and the most receptive minds in our
land were those of rejected Negroes. Color consciousness lost
some of its edge and was replaced in a large measure by class consciousness; with the rise of an integral working-class movement, a
new sense of identification came to the American Negro.

Then, for the first time since Phyllis Wheatley, the Negro began
to make a wholehearted commitment to a new world; after wan-
dering for three hundred years, he found a new sense of oneness, a
new integration; it was possible once more for him to write out of
the shared hopes and aspirations of millions of people. Phyllis
Wheatley visited the headquarters of George Washington, the
father of our republic; Langston Hughes visited the headquarters
of Lenin, the father of the Soviet Republic!

In the work of poets like Davis, Tolson, Hughes, Brown, Walker, Brooks, and Bontemps this new vision was reflected. One of the first lyrical-sounding voices of this new period was that of Langston Hughes; here, in plain images, we get, not complaints and pleas, but statements and demands:

> *Let America be America again,*
> *Let it be the dream it used to be,*
> *Let it be the pioneer in the plain,*
> *Seeking a home where he himself is free. . . .*

Out of a mood of bitter, political anger, he says:

> *Good morning, Revolution,*
> *You're the very best friend I ever had;*
> *Come on; let's pal around together . . .*

Poet Robert E. Hayden imagines the dying testimony of Gabriel, an executed slave, in these lyrical but bitter terms:

> *I see a thousand*
> *Thousand slaves*
> *Rising up*
> *From forgotten graves*
> *And their wounds drip flame*
> *On slavery's ground,*
> *And their chains shake Dixie*
> *With a thunder sound.*

> Gabriel, Gabriel
> The end is nigh,
> What do you wish
> Before you die?
> *That rebellion suckle*
> *The slave-mother's breast*
> *And black men*

> *Never, never rest*
> *Till slavery's pillars*
> *Lie splintered in dust*
> *And slavery's chains*
> *Lie eaten with rust.*

Sterling Brown hints at what the Negro would do if the numerical odds were more nearly equal:

> *They don't come [at us] by ones*
> *They don't come by twos*
> *But they come by tens*
> *They got the judges*
> *They got the lawyers*
> *They got the law*
>   *They don't come by ones*
> *They got the sheriffs*
> *They got the deputies*
>   *They don't come by twos*
> *They got the shotguns*
> *They got the rope*
>   *We get the justice*
>   *In the end*
> *And they come by tens. . . .*

Out of the Deep South, out of Texas, Melvin Tolson lifts his voice higher than that of Martin Dies and says:

> *Out of the dead-ends of poverty,*
> *Through the wilderness of Superstition,*
> *Across the barricades of Jim Crowism . . .*
> *We advance!*
> *With the peoples of the world . . .*
> *We advance!*

Margaret Walker, a Negro girl who started writing at about

the age when Phyllis Wheatley began writing, says in images that Phyllis Wheatley could not imagine:

> Let a new earth rise. Let another world be born. Let a bloody peace be written in the sky. Let a second generation full of courage issue forth, let a people loving freedom come to growth, let a beauty full of healing and a strength of final clenching be the pulsing in our spirits and our blood. Let the martial songs be written, let dirges disappear. Let a race of men now rise and take control!

Out of this sense of identification with the workers of other lands, I too wrote:

> *I am black and I have seen black hands*
> *Raised in fists of revolt, side by side with the white fists of white*
> *   workers.*
> *And some day—and it is only this which sustains me—*
> *Some day there shall be millions of them,*
> *On some red day in a burst of fists on a new horizon!*

Now, I'm not naive. I know that many of you are shaking your heads and wondering what value there is in writing like that; you may feel that we ought to write like Phyllis Wheatley, Alexander Dumas, or Alexander Pushkin. Well, we simply cannot; our world is not their world. We write out of what life gives us in the form of experience. And there is a value in what we Negro writers say. Is it not clear to you that the American Negro is the only group in our nation that consistently and passionately raises the question of freedom? This is a service to America and to the world. More than this: The voice of the American Negro is rapidly becoming the most representative voice of America and of oppressed people anywhere in the world today.

Let me remind you that during the past twenty-five years the great majority of the human race has undergone *experiences comparable to those which Negroes in* America have undergone for three centuries! These people, Russians, Germans, French, Chinese,

Indians, Danes, Spaniards, suddenly heard a voice speaking of their wrongs. From the Argentine, Brazil, Sweden, Norway, England, France, and India have come questions about the American Negro; they want to know how we live; they want our testimony since we live here amidst the greatest pretense of democracy on earth. And we Negroes are answering, straight, honestly.

So, the voice that America rejected is finding a home at last, a home such as was never dreamed of.

But our hope is steeped in a sense of sober tragedy. In the final pages of a book I wrote called *12 Million Black Voices,* I tried to indicate the quality of that hope when I said:

"We black folk, our history and our present being, are a mirror of all the manifold experiences of America. What we want, what we represent, what we endure, is what America *is.* If we black folk perish, America will perish. If America has forgotten her past, then let her look into the mirror of our consciousness and she will see the *living* past living in the present, for our memories go back, through our black folk of today, through the recollections of our black parents, and through tales of slavery told by our black grandparents, to the time when none of us, black or white, lived in this fertile land.

"The differences between black folk and white folk are not blood or color, and the ties that bind us are deeper than those that separate us. The common road of hope which we have all traveled has brought us into a stronger kinship than any words, laws, or legal claims.

"Look at us and know us and you will know yourselves, for *we* are *you,* looking back at you from the dark mirror of our lives!

"What do we black folk want?

"We want what others have, the right to share in the upward march of American life, the only life we remember or have ever known.

"The Lords of the Land say: 'We will not grant this!'

"We answer: 'We ask you to grant us nothing. We are winning our heritage, though our toll in suffering is great!' .

"The Bosses of the Buildings say: 'Your problem is beyond solution!'

"We answer: 'Our problem is being solved. We are crossing the line you dared us to cross, though we pay in the coin of death!'

"The seasons of the plantation no longer dictate the lives of many of us; hundreds of thousands of us are moving into the sphere of conscious history.

"We are with the new tide. We stand at the crossroads. We watch each new procession. The hot wires carry urgent appeals. Print compels us. Voices are speaking. Men are moving! And we shall be with them. . . ."

I am leaving off my interpretation of the literature of the American Negro at a point which antedates the present by some years. After World War II a list of new names and new themes entered the body of American Negro expression, but not enough time has elapsed for me to subject that new phase of expression to the same kind of analysis that I've used in the foregoing. Not enough perspective exists for me to feel the new trends. Yet the sheer absence of some of the old qualities is enough to allow one to draw some inferences. For example, in the work of Chester Himes, Ralph Ellison, James Baldwin, Ann Petry, Frank Yerby, Gwendolyn Brooks, etc., one finds a sharp loss of lyricism, a drastic reduction of the racial content, a rise in preoccupation with urban themes and subject matter both in the novel and the poem. Why is this?

Again I remind you that an understanding of Negro expression cannot be arrived at without a constant reference to the environment which cradles it. Directly after World War II, the United States and Soviet Russia emerged as the two dominant world powers. This meant a lessening of the influence of the ideology of Marxism in America and a frantic attempt on the part of white Americans to set their racial house somewhat in order in the face of world criticism. America's assumption of world leadership brought her racial problem to the fore in the mind of the world and the resulting shame and self-consciousness on the part of

white Americans have resulted in several dramatic alterations in
the Negro's relationship to the American scene. The recent decision of the United States Supreme Court to integrate the schools
of America on a basis of racial equality is one, but by no means
the chief, change that has come over the American outlook.
Naturally this effort on the part of the American nation to assimi-
late the Negro has had its effect upon Negro literary expression.

I've heard some people express the view that they do not like
the new literary expression of the Negro as much as they admired
the old. This is a sentimental approach. What I've discussed with
you in this lecture certainly should have proved that the mode
and pitch of Negro literary expression would alter as soon as the
attitude of the nation toward the Negro changed.

At the present moment there is no one dominant note in
Negro literary expression. As the Negro merges into the main
stream of American life, there might result actually a disappear-
ance of Negro literature as such. If that happens, it will mean that
those conditions of life that formerly defined what was "Negro"
have ceased to exist, and it implies that Negroes are Negroes
because they are treated as Negroes. Indeed, I'd say to you here
who listen to my words that I could convert any of you into
Negroes, in a psychological sense, in a period of six months. That
is, I could, by subjecting you to certain restrictions, hatreds, hos-
tilities, etc., make you express yourselves as the American Negro
formerly did.

One last thought. . . . As Negro literary expression changes,
one feels that American liberal thought has sustained a loss.
What, then, was the relation of Negro expression to liberal
thought in the United States? The Negro was a kind of conscience
to that body of liberal opinion. The liberals were ridden with a
sense of guilt, and the Negro's wailing served as something that
enabled the liberal to define his relationship to the American
scene. Today the relationship between liberals and Negroes is hard
to define. Indeed, one feels that the liberals kind of resent the new
trend of independence which the Negro exhibits. But this is
inevitable; the Negro, as he learns to stand on his own feet and

express himself not in purely racial, but human terms, will launch criticism upon his native land which made him feel a sense of estrangement that he never wanted. This new attitude could have a healthy effect upon the culture of the United States. At long last, maybe a merging of Negro expression with American expression will take place. As that process develops and continues, you may watch it, using the few concepts that I've discussed with you. In that case I feel that its human drama will have, perhaps, some meaning for you.

If the expression of the American Negro should take a sharp turn toward strictly racial themes, then you will know by that token that we are suffering our old and ancient agonies at the hands of our white American neighbors. If, however, our expression broadens, assumes the common themes and burdens of literary expression which are the heritage of all men, then by that token you will know that a humane attitude prevails in America towards us. And a gain in humaneness in America is a gain in humaneness for us all. When that day comes, there will exist one more proof of the oneness of man, of the basic unity of human life on this earth.

4

The Miracle of Nationalism in the African Gold Coast

TIME: *The middle of the twentieth century.*

PLACE: *The hot and lush high rain forest of British West Africa.*

CHARACTERS: *Black students, black workers, black doctors, black judges, black knights of the British Empire, black merchants, black schoolteachers, black politicians, black mothers, black cooks, black intellectuals, detribalized and disinherited; and a white British colonial Governor, white merchants and businessmen, white British civil servants, white missionaries, white British army officers, and white CID men.*

I've commenced as though I were about to present a drama. But it's not quite that. Yet, in a sense, what I'm about to relate is a phase of the prime, central, and historical drama of the twentieth century, the most common and exciting drama that we know. All of us are caught up in its stupendous and complicated unfolding; all of us play some kind of role, passive or active, in it; and yet most of us are totally unaware that we do so.

What I have to tell you shall be in the form of a story, a simple story. That is, the story is simple in outline, but its scope and meaning and content are extremely intricate. What makes this story even more involved than the telling of it is that, though it deals in the main with black people in the faraway depths of Africa's fetid jungles, though it is about life couched in a strange guise, though it's about men whose skin color and whose shape of nostrils and whose curl of hair and whose accents of speech and whose outlook upon life differ drastically and markedly from yours, this story involves you, you white men of Europe; it is, in an odd sense, *your* story—a tale of yourselves projected in a drama whose setting is fantastic and whose characters are draped in external aspects of life alien to you. As you watch this story unfold and roll toward its unexpected denouement, you will be observing actions whose motives are akin to yours, attitudes mainly derived from your assumptions, decisions whose resolutions partake of your will, and ideals whose emotional coloration reflect values that have long shone in the ardent hearts of Western man. Indeed, I'd go so far as to say that, had you been the personages in this drama, you would undoubtedly have acted more or less as these black men acted. In fact, I'm sure that, had it not been for your historical attitudes and deeds, and the historical attitudes and deeds of your fathers and your fathers' fathers, this story would not have happened.

One swelteringly hot night, in 1948, a group of six black men, each coming stealthily from his home and traveling by a separate, secret route, met at an agreed-upon spot in an African jungle. All six of these men were members of what was then called the United Gold Coast Convention, a nationalist organization composed almost exclusively of the black bourgeoisie, that is, black doctors, black merchants, black lawyers, black businessmen, etc., who resided in an area of British West Africa which Europeans had fondly christened, because of the fabulous booty in gold and slaves that it had yielded them, the "Gold Coast."

The avowed aim of that organization was self-government. Under the justification that it was allowing the Gold Coast people to prepare themselves for eventual nationhood, the British permitted this organization to exist more or less legally, though no one could really tell how long the organization would be tolerated or at what point it would or could be characterized by the British CID (Criminal Investigation Division of Scotland Yard) as Communistic or subversive.

The six men meeting clandestinely in that jungle that night, though members of the organization, were in deep and passionate disagreement with that organization's aims. They were ex-tribal men and they felt that that organization was too snobbish, too British in tone and outlook, too hedged about with property, educational, social, and class qualifications. In short, they felt that it was a kind of exclusive club. Though that organization's membership consisted entirely of *black* men, these six blacks felt that it fostered values, attitudes, and standards alien and offensive to their hearts, that is, *British* values of extreme individualism, of invidious class and social distinctions, of divisive Anglo-Saxon manners that facilitated British tactics of divide and rule. They resented being told from the *outside* what was "good" for them; they felt outraged at the thought of someone above them monitoring the pace and pitch of their social, economic, and political progress. They wanted the right to choose what they felt they needed most and they were convinced that their wisdom was better for their people than the cold, dry, abstract notions of professors in British universities. These men knew that the Western world considered those aspects of the tribal life of their country that most resembled Western mores as "good" and those aspects that differed from Western mores as "bad."

Though these men wore Western clothes, they had not learned—and did not wish to learn—to look down in disfavor upon the naked, ignorant tribal masses that comprised their racial, cultural, and blood kin. They were of the conviction that the struggle to free their country from alien rule should involve the whole population—every man, woman, and child in it regardless of religious, family, or class loyalties—and not just the black, British-educated elite. These six black men were, therefore, as much opposed to the rich British blacks as they were to the rich British whites. They wanted freedom, their own flag flying over their ancestral homeland, the right to restore the ancient names of their land, their towns, their rivers. In short, they wanted the right to control their total destiny, and they wanted that right for more than just a few of their kind who had been hand-picked by Britishers actuated by racial, religious, and imperialistic motives. To be sure, these six blacks had read attentively their John Stuart Mill, their John Locke; but there was something in their hearts that made them detached from, and suspicious of, the preachments and postulates of those British prophets of freedom and democracy.

So the gathering together that night of these six men in secret constituted an act of treason not only toward the British, but toward a decisive section of their own people, the best qualified and wisest of their own leaders. What did the six men want? They were striving for a total transformation and redemption of the situation in which they found themselves. They were politicians, these men, but their policies, because of the situation in which they found themselves and because of their peculiar outlook upon life, bordered upon the intensity of the religious.

No record was kept of that meeting that night in that jungle, but, since I've talked to all of the men involved and feel I know them, I think I can paraphrase what they said. Will you allow me to state their case, using my memory and imagination to put words in their mouths?

Black Man Number One:

"I want no freedom based upon the assumptions of the British.

Such a freedom simply means exchanging a set of white masters for a set of black masters. If I'm against British rule, then I'm against the rule of her stooges."

Black Man Number Two:

"All day and all night they talk to us about 'sound and solid development, sound and solid education.' All right. The British, in 104 years, provided an abortive sort of education for less than 10 per cent of our people; that is, less than 10 per cent of our population received an elementary and badly taught knowledge of reading, writing, and arithmetic. Now, if that British educational timetable were followed by the black bourgeois elite when it came to power, it would take one thousand years to make our society partially literate. I say to hell with John Stuart Mill and John Locke. Let's make our own philosophy, based upon our *own* needs.

"Who says that we black men must duplicate and ape the development of the white man? Aren't we in the position of studying the white man's mistakes, taking advantage of them, and making even faster progress than he made? To imitate the white man means that we are still slaves in our hearts. I say, let us be free; and freedom means mapping out our own road for ourselves, making our own mistakes and being responsible for them."

Black Man Number Three:

"Since more than 90 per cent of our people are illiterate, it cannot be said that Britain has any loyal masses in the Gold Coast. Why, then, is she here? She wants the bauxite, the gold, the timber, the manganese, the diamonds. I say, let's so organize our people and so pool these raw materials that we can bargain them for what we need most from the outer world. Why in hell should white men come in here and take our raw materials at prices that *they set,* and then sell us imported European goods at prices that *they determine?"*

Black Man Number Four:

"How are we going to organize our people? As the European Socialist organizers organized theirs? Or as the Russian Communists organized and trained their people for revolution? Obviously not. We have practically no industrial proletariat and, hence, Marxist ideology is, in the long run, of little or no interest to us. I say let us organize our people on the basis of a struggle for national freedom and of their being proud of their ancestor-worshiping traditions. Now, gentlemen, I realize that we do not believe in such mumbo jumbo, and all the childish rituals that such traditions imply. But we have no other basis upon which to make a call for unity. So we must say to our people: 'Let's heave out the British and save our culture and traditions.' But we, we who have been educated in the West, know well that the moment we start organizing our people to defend and protect their ancient traditions, those traditions must of necessity begin to weaken, will be destroyed. And that is exactly what we want. So let us do two things at once: Organize the tribes and pit them in struggle against the British, and, in organizing our tribes to do that job, we launch them toward taking the first step toward a secular life, toward a new outlook."

Black Man Number Five:

"I agree. We are *outsiders* in our own land. So let us stand *outside* of the tribal life, in which we do not believe, and organize it. That means that, in order to go forward, we must go backward a step or two. We must all, from this night forward, doff our Western clothes and wear the clothes of our tribes. We must do this in order to win the confidence and allegiance of the masses. But we must go further than that; we must cut off the avenue of retreat to the past so that our people will *never* go back, *can* never go back. Though dressed in tribal clothes, we must always use the most modern methods in organizing. We are going to latch our tribal people directly onto the techniques of the twentieth century. We're going to *change* our people!"

Black Man Number Six:

"We need really fear no competition from outsiders, from potential rivals, such as Communists. During the last fifty years there has not come from Russia one volume dealing with the manner and techniques of organizing tribal men. So let us make our main slogan: SELF-GOVERNMENT NOW! In that way, no one can top our appeal to our people. One other thing. We must have unity. We must have an iron discipline. He who breaks the unity of our ranks will have to be tossed beyond the pale. The basis for that is already in our tribal life. It is not only a political party that we must organize; it is a brotherhood. We must share and share alike in all things. So tight must our unity be that no enemy can sneak into our ranks. The whole might of Britain cannot break a political unity based upon tribal brotherhood and cemented in blood loyalty."

That must have been how much of the discussion went. These men were desperately angry and serious. The hot emotions that bubbled in their hearts bordered upon violence, made them tense and anxious. Their impulses were turgid and blind. Yet, despite their fury, their manner was controlled, calm. These men were spiritually homeless and they were ardently seeking a home for their hearts.

But there were no fetish priests present. The traditional big black pot with a roaring fire beneath it, the kind of pot which white Westerners like to imagine that missionaries are parboiled in, was absent from that jungle meeting. These black men did not even believe in spirits; indeed, they didn't even lend credence to what is popularly called the "Other World." The truth is that these six desperate black men were all educated products of Western universities; upon all of them had been conferred degrees in law, literature, and political science from the universities of France, England, and America. Why, then, were they angry? Why were they meeting secretly in the dead of the night in a jungle where the only sounds were the muted cries of wild beasts?

These men were meeting to plot what they felt to be the freedom of their country, their nation. What? What "nation"? What "country"? When were there ever nations in Black Africa? History dimly tells us that maybe there existed some few Sudanic black kingdoms some hundreds of years ago, but surely no black nations in the modern sense of that term existed in Africa in historically recent times. Then what did these six black men mean by the "freedom of their country," their "nation"?

You can see that, from the outset, this simple story takes on historical, cultural, and psychological complexities and obscurities. From where did these six black men ever get the notion of building something that had never existed before in Africa? Were they irrational? Were they dreaming? Or were they merely wishing? It was infinitely more recondite than that. But, even so, did not their sanguine desire for nationhood clash mockingly with the impersonal, indifferent jungle density that lay all about them? Was not there something ironically incongruous in their yearning to belong to a modern nation when their black brothers and sisters, millions upon millions of them, lay sleeping a sleep that was sounder than that sleep of which dreams form the mysterious curtain?—a sleep of ancestor-worshiping religion which made their invisible fathers, long dead, more real and more powerful than the earth upon which they walked—that earth which they tilled—that earth that sustained them from day to day? How foolhardy were these six men, lonely and glutted with bitter pride, to dare even to think of pitting themselves against the mental crystallizations of thousands of years! Who were their friends? Surely not the British, not the Western businessmen, not the Protestant or Catholic missionaries. And who were their allies? Surely not the Communists, for the Communists had long ago adamantly decreed that there had to exist an industrial proletariat to lead the revolution. Who understood them? The sociologists? If so, I've yet to read an account from them of how these men really feel. The psychoanalysts? Vaguely, perhaps, but surely not in terms of any concreteness that would serve to make their turbulent state of mind sympathetically known. What audacity did these six black men have to think of challenging the deep-rooted traditions which even white missionaries and white social scientists of the Western world had failed to change or modify during long centuries of effort? Don Quixote was a sane and balanced man compared to these six black revolutionaries!

But, stop and think a moment. Their dreaming and plotting for the "freedom of their country" flew into the face of even sterner realities than the religion of their people. These men lived in the

Gold Coast, an area about the size of England; it was administered by a much-vaunted British civil service behind which, protecting it, was the ever-present threat of force represented by British district commissioners, soldiers, police, etc. And, beyond this show of force, lurked the British navy and army, which could, upon the whim of a moment's notice, change the government or suspend the constitution. The stealthy British CID was omnipresent, smelling out the least vestiges of subversion.

How in the name of common sense, then, could these six black men, unarmed and penniless, even think of establishing a nation of their own in the teeth of British opposition and the stagnant traditions of their own people? What an absurdity! Were they not like unto children? One laughed at men like that. Or one pitied them. They would never succeed. Their situation was more than hopeless. Hadn't they better come to terms with their people, quell their hot passions, obey the wisdom of the British and live peaceful, useful, good, sound lives? Why attempt the impossible? Oughtn't they progress slowly, soundly, according to the way in which the Western world had progressed? Oughtn't they to think of taking decades to build a nation, yea, centuries even?

Yes, these men knew all of these cogent arguments, but they had long ago firmly decided that they could no longer wait. They were being prompted and spurred by elements, strange and compounded, that lay deep in their own personalities. They were hungering for something that had not come into reality and they had gotten the impulse of that hunger from the white men who had ruled them, from the white missionaries, the white military, the white mercenary—the three white groups which the Asians and Africans call the three M's of imperialism. These six men had been swept out of the orbit of influence of their tribal life and into the sphere, no matter how loosely, of the Western world. At long last the colonizing efforts of your forefathers were bearing their strange fruit. Hence, these men, though black, were not really, in a strict sense of the word, traditional Africans at all. They were black and they lived in Africa; but, at heart, they were really more akin to Europe than to Africa. Their outlook upon the world and their feel of life had been toned by Western values.

If we are prepared to understand how Westernized these six black men were—and their Westernization would have to differ profoundly from yours, for they had become Westernized under corrosive conditions of partial servitude—then we are ready to understand something else about them that is even more surprising.

These men were caught in a psychological trap; they were living in a situation in which they did not really belong. They had been plucked by the hand of the white man out of their tribal societies, educated in Western institutions, and then thrown back into the jungle to sink or swim. They knew the West from the *outside;* and now they saw and felt their own society from the *outside*. They shared a third but not quite yet clearly defined point of view.

Living the daily life of the tribe and with their heads filled with Western values, these men saw the Gold Coast in what light? To understand how they saw life, you must open your minds and imagination. Though the guns of the British navy and the tanks of the British army were pitted against their aspirations, and though the stagnant traditions of their people loomed as an almost insuperable barrier to the realization of their demands, these men, from the angle of vision afforded by their unique position, saw something in the structure of the society of the Gold Coast colony that made the task that they had in mind much easier and simpler than you would suppose.

True, they knew that they could not face the invincible might of the British army, navy, and air force and win. That was out of the question. And they knew well that the ancient traditions of their people were strong and deeply entrenched. But these men, as I have said, were Westernized. THEY HAD ANALYZED THE RELATION OF BRITAIN TO THEIR ANCESTRAL HOME-LAND. They knew exactly where Britain was strong and where she was weak, how British minds worked and what British values were. They knew how to distinguish between what the British said and what they really meant; standing *outside* of Britain, they knew the sharp difference between British professions of idealism and British behavior. They had long grown used to hearing the British say one thing and do the opposite. They knew, at bottom, that the British respected only strength, would react, in the main, only to a *fait accompli.* They were no fools, these black men; they were hard, tough; and they were willing to sacrifice their very lives to test the validity of the reality that they had discovered through Western instrumentalities of thought.

As we know, the population of the colony was more than 90 per cent illiterate. In the urban parts of the colony, due to Western influence, there had set in a deep and chronic disorganization of family tribal life, and the British, who had wrought this atomization of family life, seemed happily ignorant of it. Hence, there existed large masses of tribal individuals who owed no deep allegiances to anybody or anything—masses that were free to be organized—masses that constituted an ironic British gift to the black national revolutionary. And the traditional tribal structure, though intact as a functioning frame of emotional reference from day to day, had been dealt a mortal blow by the religious, mercantile, and military interests of the West. In sum, a kind of void, emotional and psychological in nature, existed in the social structure, and only a few Africans, even, seemed aware of it.

But, ah, you may say, you are overlooking something of vital importance. Britain is strong in Africa because of the work, sacrificial and dedicated, of her many missionaries. Christianity has friends among the masses of Africans.

Well, maybe yes and maybe no. Let's take a quick and close look and see how Christian values resided in the tribal heart. The first thing to be noticed is that the very essence of the African drive for nationalism stemmed from the influence of Christianity itself! Had the missionary not gone meddling in Africa, the mores of the millions of blacks would have remained intact. What the missionary failed to do was replace effectively what he had torn out of the African heart. That void that he had created could be felt in all of its terrible intensity only by the African who endured it, and it was that African who was now moving resolutely toward setting his emotional house in order.

Before the coming of the missionary, the African's tribal life had been wholly religious; the introduction of Christianity had reduced the volume, if I may be permitted to put it that way, of religion, not increased it. Hence, the African's contact with Christianity had freed him for action. But what kind of action? That was the question. So these black Christian friends of Britain were filled with ambivalence; they felt that they had been seduced by Britain and then abandoned by her, and now they hated her as much as they loved her.

The white missionaries, the white military, and the white mercenaries, because of racial antipathies, kept apart from the natives, refusing to live or mingle with them on a basis of social equality. And the few educated blacks who collaborated with the British also lived aloof from their own black brothers. The white British civil service, in which a few qualified blacks participated, also quarantined itself from the native population. Thus, upon the most casual inspection, more than 90 per cent of the native population lived remote from the British. Psychologically, Britain existed somewhere on Mars as far as the native Gold Coaster was concerned. Britain was an image, dim and misty, or completely non-existent, in their minds. Even to say that 90 per cent of the population was loyal or disloyal to Britain was to talk in terms of unrealities. The truth is that the masses of the Gold Coast people didn't feel anything for or against Britain; they lived, labored, procreated, and died. This stagnant state of affairs was called *Pax Britannica,* and it had been most carefully, deliberately, and profitably arranged.

Why was Britain, then, in the Gold Coast at all, since her relationship to the bulk of the population was so tenuous and remote? I'll answer that question, though I know that my answer will make many of you bristle. And I'll tell you what those six black revolutionaries thought and felt about why Britain was there. The absolute consensus of attitude of the black life in the Gold Coast, Left and Right, Christian and pagan, insurgent and conservative, was that Britain was there to get what she could of the natural resources of the colony. These six black men did not contemplate this bald and cynical fact with any degree of hate or bitterness; the awful thing was that they were calm about it; it seemed natural to them that Britain should do this, and a British education had enabled them to arrive at this negative interpretation of Britain's role. Were these black men, then, aware of any contradiction in Britain's attitude toward them? They were. One African explained his bafflement about the British by saying:

"They send us to universities and urge us to study, but the moment they grant us a degree, they become afraid of us."

Another young African expressed himself as follows:

"They continuously stress that we become qualified, but when we become qualified, they tell us that they like the uneducated native better, that the naked tribal man is noble and unspoiled."

But why had Britain bothered to educate a few Africans in the Gold Coast at all? Should not these blacks have felt grateful for that British effort? Strangely, they felt no such thing. They had intuitively grasped that there was something odd about the desire of the British missionary to remold their minds into the patterns of white men's minds. The missionaries had explained that their preoccupation with the native was prompted by "love," and the African, living a deeply communal existence, had never been able to fathom that aloof, nervous, and condescending "love." They sensed that it was a self-centered concentration of the white man upon himself rather than upon them that caused him to propound his doctrines. In short, they felt a kind of psychological selfishness and guilt in the white man. Now, you can be sure that the British felt no such selfishness or guilt, but I'm only informing you what the blacks felt about it, and how they felt is the decisive thing here. You're entitled to your view and the blacks are certainly entitled to theirs.

The first step, therefore, that these six black men resolved to take was to deny to Britain the right to take the raw materials from the colony. A tall order, that, for six black penniless men to execute. Yet, a further analysis of the relation of Britain to the Gold Coast quickly revealed that, though that task was difficult and improbable, it was not at all impossible. These six black men knew their Marxism, but it is important to remember that they were not really Marxists. They handled Marxist thought self-consciously, standing *outside* of it, so to speak; they used it as an instrumentality to analyze reality, to make it meaningful, manageable. (But the moment they felt that that Marxist thought was no longer useful, the time when it no longer applied to their problems, they could drop it. Marxist ideology was a tool to them, a tool to be used and then cast aside. Need I remind you again that these men were *free* in their hearts? By enslaving them, Britain had liberated them. These men did not regard any system of ideas as creeds in which one had to believe; ideas were weapons, techniques. Ah, you British Prime Ministers, do you think you are masters of reality, of men? You must need have such confidence, or your empire building could not have been done. But life is more complicated than even a British Prime Minister thinks! You set out to civilize men and you produced personality types never hinted at even in your nightmares.) The Achilles' heel of Britain in the Gold Coast was, according to the analysis of these black nationalists, economic, and, if they could only somehow bruise that economic heel, half of their battle would be won.

Oh, do you suspect the cunning hand of Moscow here? If you do, you only confirm that your conditioning and reactions are traditional, popular, and natural. When the British—to anticipate my story a bit—heard of what these six black men proposed to do, they sent in their CID spies to rout out all the Red cells that could be found. For long months the CID searched, questioned, censored the mails, imposed curfews, and probed, but not a single Red cell did it discover.

But how could these six black men paralyze the economic life of the Gold Coast and deny to Britain the raw materials that she wanted? Well, again, a most casual analysis of the relation of the British to the native revealed fatal weak spots. The only good roads that existed in the colony ran from the mines and timber mills to the seaports, and there were but few of them. And the actual number of loyal, educated blacks in the colony was some few score. In the last analysis, the relation of Britain to the Gold Coast depended upon the functioning loyalty of these few score. It was as delicate as that. Suppose, then, that those few score black bourgeois men were discredited, were driven from their positions of influence and favor, what would happen? The answer was so simple as to be startling. The British would be compelled to depend upon those tough-minded revolutionary blacks, whether they liked them or not, who had organized and thus had control of the native masses. So the strategy was obvious: Knock out the few educated bourgeois blacks who were loyal to the white British administrators, and those administrators would then be faced with a mass of four and a half million tribal blacks many of whom could not even speak English and whose loyalty was more to their dead fathers than to the power of Britain. The British would then be faced with a choice: They would either have to deal with the new spokesmen of these four and a half million tribal-minded men, or shoot their spokesmen and then rule the black masses by sheer naked force.

But can bombs produce cocoa? Can machine guns cut timber? Can bayonets dig the gold out of the mines? Can tanks unearth the bauxite? The answer to these questions was the crux of what those six black men had to decide that night in the jungle, and they decided that Britain badly, desperately, needed the gold, the timber, the bauxite. They guessed right. For, when the chips were down, the British said: "Let's talk business." The British turned their backs upon poor Jesus Christ hanging there upon the Cross and took out their fountain pens and sat down at tables with the black revolutionary leaders and began to add, divide, subtract, and multiply.

Now I come to an odd part of my story. Those six sweating black men in that jungle, discussing and planning and plotting the freedom of a nation that did not exist, resolved to bind themselves together; they agreed to call themselves: *The Secret Circle.*[*] Then they swore fetish, a solemn oath on the blood of their ancestors to avoid women, alcohol, and all pleasure until their "country" was free and the Union Jack no longer flew over their land. They swore fetish to stick together.

What? Fetish? Ah, you will say: "These black men were not as Western as you claimed." Yes, they swore fetish. Well, why not? They were scared of the British. They were scared of their own people—their brothers and sisters who would not understand what they were trying to do. And, above all, they were scared of one another. Suppose one of their number informed the British of what they were planning? All of them would either be killed or imprisoned. Hence, though Westernized, these men swore a blood oath to stick together, not to betray one another. We now come to a twilight zone in my story, a zone that will make the reality here more complicated still. I have contended that these men were Westernized. They were. But they lived amidst tribal conditions of life and they reacted to ancestor-worshiping values each day. Thus their world was compounded half of Europe and half of Africa. When they desired to see reality in terms of its external and objective aspects, they thought and felt Western; when they had to deal with their own emotions, they felt and thought African. They lived in two worlds. BUT THEY DIDN'T REALLY AND DEEPLY BELIEVE IN EITHER OF THOSE WORLDS. THE WORLD THAT THEY REALLY WANTED, THE WORLD THAT WOULD BE THE HOME OF THEIR HEARTS, HAD NOT YET COME INTO BEING. So, while standing *outside* of both worlds, so to speak, they were manipulating aspects of both worlds to create the one and single world that they really wanted.

Now I know that you've heard that, when you educate an

---

[*]In *Black Power* (Harper & Brothers, New York: 1954), in which the author rendered an account of the nationalistic revolution in the Gold Coast, all mention or description of this highly interesting and indigenous African political cell was deliberately withheld for fear that the politically reactionary or ideologically immature would confuse it with Russian Communism and call for the suppression of the African's first modern bid for freedom.

R. W.

African, he talks like a European but feels like an African still. White racists contend that a Western education with an African goes only skin deep. All of this is much too simple. The African, when educated in the West, is really neither European nor African. The truth is that he has yet to make himself into what he is to be. So there is really nothing so astonishing about our six black men swearing a blood oath to be loyal to one another; it is no more astonishing than when Western white men cross themselves just before they send a bombing mission to seize the Suez Canal, or when the President of the United States gets on his knees and prays to God just before he issues the order to drop the atom bomb on Hiroshima. Both the African and the white Westerner are partly rational and partly irrational: that is, all men are somewhat infantile. The other man's God is our devil, and our God is usually his devil. What makes other men seem outlandish to us is our lack of imagination. We all, both black and white, both Easterners and Westerners, have our blind spots. Conditions of life shape our attitudes and give us our values.

This incongruity, this mixing of tribal and Western values, runs like a red thread through the whole story I'm to tell you. Watch this curious intertwining of tradition with modernity; study these Western blacks dealing self-consciously with their tribal religions; contemplate polygamy blending with puritanism; marvel at the sprouting of socialist thought in a jungle where no working-class ideology existed to support it; try to grasp this strange transition of politics turning into a passion whose intensity partook of the religious.

My story of Gold Coast nationalism can now run swiftly, for I'm reasonably sure that you sense or feel the substratum of emotion, idealism, and self-vindication out of which this nationalism was forged. In most discussions of movements of this sort, you'll hear descriptions of constitutions, of the principles of democracy, etc. In short, you'll hear Westerners, who feel that only their assumptions are valid for all people, at all times, and everywhere, tell you how the lower orders of mankind are gradually beginning to resemble them. In contrast to that approach, I emphasize the

primal impulses that give birth to such movements toward freedom. I'm telling this story, if you don't mind, from the black
man's point of view.

One of the men who comprised *The Secret Circle* was named
Nkrumah. Educated both in Britain and America, he had been
sent for by the heads of the United Gold Coast Convention to act
as secretary, and it was he who objected most strongly to the
snobbish and reactionary leanings of the educated black elite.
Resolved now upon a course of bold action to organize the energies of the entire population, Nkrumah launched a drive to
broaden the basis of the United Gold Coast Convention.
Nkrumah became the leader of *The Secret Circle.* How did that
happen? Did he declare himself as leader and impose himself
upon them? No. His followers declared him leader. Naturally, he
was qualified for this role by his superb organizing and speaking
abilities; but, by his colleagues fastening their hopes upon him, he
was lifted to the position of almost a deity. Listen carefully to
what I'm explaining and perhaps you'll get some insight into the
tendencies toward, and origins of, authoritarian or dictatorship
governments. The concrete nature of the situation throws up such
phenomena. The "cult of the personality" was not invented in
Moscow. The longing for someone to be The Leader stems from
the very nature of the human material involved. We can say that
Nkrumah and his talent for leadership were captured by his followers. He could not say yes or no. These masses needed someone
upon whom they could project their hopes, and Nkrumah was
chosen. There came moments when, had he refused to act, they
would have killed him. Do you recall the story of the Dying God?
Gods must serve men, or they are killed.

Nkrumah's labor to strengthen the popular basis of the United
Gold Coast Convention coincided with the spontaneous efforts
of a subchief (of a tiny state called Ga) to lower the price of
imported goods. Early in 1948 a colony-wide boycott was
launched against foreign merchants. Now, let me explain that the
boycott against foreign merchants and the efforts of Nkrumah

were not allied. They were independent ventures, but both were heading in the same direction. This is not going to be the last time that I shall call your attention to spontaneous factors leaping up from the life of the Gold Coast natives and coinciding with the leadership of Nkrumah. More than anything else, these spontaneous features of support proved to *The Secret Circle* that they were headed in the right direction, that their analysis of Gold Coast reality was correct. One had only to give a determined push against the structure of political and economic rule of the British and that rule went toppling.

The boycott was effective and, within one month, the European business firms were on their knees. The members of the Government and the heads of European business firms met and pledged an immediate reduction in the retail prices of imported goods. But, during the days that followed, when the populace went shopping in the stores that sold imported goods and naively expected to find a reduction in retail prices, they found the old prices intact. A mounting anger swept the colony. Spontaneous demonstrations flared against the firms selling European goods. In the afternoon of February 28, 1948, a delegation of ex-servicemen, chanting slogans and waving banners, marched on the Governor's castle in Christianborg to present their grievances. The police ordered the demonstrators to disperse and they refused. The police opened fire and killed three black veterans of British campaigns in India and Burma. The news of this killing spread, and an infuriated populace began to loot the foreign firms. Arson and street fighting ensued and, during the following days, violence gripped the southern half of the colony. Twenty-nine people were killed and about two hundred and thirty-seven were injured.

From this it seems that the analysis of the reality of the Gold Coast made by *The Secret Circle* was sound. They had not discussed democracy; they had not talked of trial by jury; they had not debated the merits of free speech. They had assumed that they and their people were being cheated, that the whole of their lives had been caught in an economic trap which allowed the

British to buy from them at low prices and sell to them at high prices! And the moment the finger of *The Secret Circle* touched that sore spot, an explosion resulted.

And what did the British think of all this? It was all a plot sponsored by the men in Moscow, of course. Surely the nobility of their intentions could not set off reactions of hate and violence of that magnitude. Therefore, find the Red culprit! They, the British, were doing good, saving the heathen, uplifting fallen humanity, etc. So find the devils who were meddling with their civilizing mission!

The Governor declared a state of emergency. A curfew was imposed. The leaders of the United Gold Coast Convention sent cables to London petitioning the British Colonial Secretary to create a commission of inquiry to study the underlying causes of the disorders; they also demanded an interim government. The Governor countered this move by arresting the leaders of the United Gold Coast Convention and banishing them to the barren Northern Territories where they were incarcerated separately for fear that they would meet and plot. But the British had never really understood the mentality of the people they were governing; the black leaders immediately called upon the loyalty of their black guards and established instant communication with one another and their followers. The tribal brotherhood forged by *The Secret Circle* was proving too much for the British. Another government, as yet unrecognized and invisible, had come to exist in the Gold Coast and the British were oblivious of its reality and power. Yet they were alarmed, and feared that the local black soldiers and police were not loyal, so they imported troops from Nigeria.

As a result of the appeals made by the new revolutionary leadership, the core of which was *The Secret Circle*, the British Colonial Secretary in London appointed a commission to investigate the causes of the sudden flare-up in violence and to recommend constructive measures. The commission was named after its chairman, Aiken Watson, and it took testimony in April of 1948; the arrested leaders were released so that they could give evidence. In June of that year the commission issued a report that declared the old constitution outmoded, urged a new constitution embodying the aspirations of the people, and endorsed a ministerial type of government patterned on those obtaining in the dominions. Thus, the commission confirmed the diagnosis of Gold Coast reality that had been made by *The Secret Circle.*

But, when the Governor, in December 1948, appointed a constitutional committee of forty Africans under the chairmanship of a famous black jurist, the now Sir Henley Coussey, apprehension set in. The constitutional committee was composed entirely of upper-class chiefs and lawyers, and the younger nationalist elements of the population were completely ignored. The pattern of British class snobbery that *The Secret Circle* so loathed was about to be saddled upon them again in a new manner. Nkrumah's immediate following urged him to leave the United Gold Coast Convention and set up a rival organization that would embody the real aims and feelings of the masses. But Nkrumah hesitated. He did not wish to split the unity of the people.

When the constitutional committee began its work on the twentieth of January 1949, trade unionists, students, the women traders of the streets, and the nationalist elements launched a vehement protest against the exclusion of their representatives. Nkrumah hastily organized a committee of youths and sent a team of young men touring the country to raise three demands: (1) universal adult suffrage; (2) a fully elected legislature with a fully representative cabinet; and (3) collective ministerial responsibility.

The fat was in the fire. Naturally these demands were beyond the aims of the black bourgeois leaders of the United Gold Coast Convention. And Nkrumah had been pushed by his followers to take this extreme step. He had had either to take it or forfeit his leadership; though the leader, he was really a kind of captive, a prisoner of the hopes and passions of his people. This is an important point to remember, for all else in this story—and its aftermath has yet to be enacted—rests upon it or will be influenced by it. Politics in these non-Western societies proceeds in a manner quite unknown to us where wages, parties, newspapers, printing, plumbing, and public opinion shape the deeds of men.

The rich black doctors, lawyers, and politicians reacted with fury, as was to be expected. What was this man, Nkrumah, doing? The naked ignorant masses had no part in politics and government. The right to vote, they argued, ought to be conditioned by how much money or property you had, for money and property indicated how much you knew, how dependable and responsible you were. Hadn't John Stuart Mill and John Locke said so? And was not England great as proof of what Mill and Locke had said? Who would dare gainsay the august wisdom of the savants of the mighty British? A tramp like Nkrumah and his wild-eyed boys of the streets of the disorganized harbor towns? How absurd! But they failed to take action against Nkrumah in time, for they were convinced that, if they only talked to him in a fatherly manner, he would change. These rich and sedate blacks were the psychological prisoners of their assumptions; they felt that even the sun agreed that their ideas were the only good and valid ones. They enjoined Nkrumah to stop his agitating, and Nkrumah, deciding to cast his lot with his people, countered by going even further into radical departures. In his newspaper, *The Accra Evening News,* which had been launched in September 1948, he vehemently demanded a democratic constitution. The rich blacks reaffirmed their disdain for the masses. The differences could not be bridged. Nkrumah, urged by his supporters, resigned from the United Gold Coast Convention and launched and announced, in August 1949, the Convention People's Party and stated his intention of staging "Positive Action" based on non-violence—a political stroke that fitted the mood of the country.

It was a gesture that called for tribal unity, brotherhood, sacrifice, and a rebirth of the ancient sense of the people's continuity of being in its traditional form. But, at the same time, Nkrumah announced the following modern socialistic aims: Housing, technical education, road building, health measures to reduce infantile mortality, the liberation of women from traditional fetters, the building of co-operatives, and a campaign of mass education to wipe out illiteracy. A mixture, eh? It was. The tribal traditions were emphasized at the very moment when they were being orga-

nized toward goals that would eventually nullify them! No wonder the British and the rich blacks were dizzy with bewilderment.
The ancient national dress of the Gold Coast, togas draped about
the body in Roman style, was worn with a new pride now in
every village and street of the country. And yet the methods of
urging the population to struggle for national freedom and socialism were couched in terms of fleets of trucks with loudspeakers,
brass bands, pamphlets, and mass meetings where oxen were sac-
rificially slain to appease the spirits of the dead ancestors! The
chiefs, under their brilliant umbrellas, dribbled palm wine and
gin upon the earth as they recited libations to the departed in the
name of socialism! Men with six wives came forward and saluted
and endorsed a social order that would reduce the number of
their wives to only one! (Yet these men had no intention of giving
up their many wives.) Women, hitherto regarded as chattels,
came out of their compound kitchens and danced and sang in the
streets. The Gold Coast African greeted the dawn of the twentieth century in his community by pounding his tom-toms with
wild frenzy.

Disorder? Irrationality? Foolishness? The antics of children?
No wonder the British recoiled with consternation, and no wonder the rich black nationalists sided with the British in sheer horror and fear. But let us take a closer look at this disorder, this irrationality, this foolishness, these antics of children. *What else could
have happened but what did happen?*

In terms of Western assumptions, there existed no foundations
for classical democracy in the Gold Coast; that is, if one defined
democracy only and merely as a voting choir of literate property
owners who believed that there was only one God, only one
Jesus, and only one Holy Ghost. That, in all honesty, has to be
admitted. But, in 104 years of British rule, and during a stretch
of historic time dating back to the fifteenth century, France,
Denmark, Sweden, Germany, and Portugal had held sway over
the people of the Gold Coast and had made no effort to establish
any such foundations for democracy. Hence, the easiest criticism
to hurl today at the inhabitants of the Gold Coast is: "You are not

ready for self-government!" And the Gold Coaster can reply: "Whether we are ready or not, in accordance with your notions, is not important. We're acting." And that is exactly what Nkrumah had decided to do.

Nkrumah was—and all the basic facts were with him—proceeding upon the assumption that the subjective lives of his people had been smashed, that the missionaries had rendered the lives of his people meaningless, that the merchants had trapped them in a manner that rendered them more and more impoverished, emotionally and materially, each day, and that the guns of the British, though they were there in the name of public order, were weapons that intimidated the very foundations of the personalities of the people toward whom they were pointed. Nkrumah's drive for self-government was more than merely a scheme to grab selfishly at the reins of political power. It was a mandate to his people that they were not intrinsically inferior, no matter what their present condition of life was, to the rest of the human race—an implication that British rule had long sought to implant in them. More, Nkrumah gave sanction to his people that, though their outlook upon life and their tribal customs differed drastically from those of the Western white man, their customs and outlook did not justify their being conquered and held abjectly as economic hostages for centuries. He encouraged his people to believe that, though they were lagging behind in the race for progress, they needed no *outside* tutors to intimidate them with guns while monitoring their daily lives.

What was, then, Nkrumah's task? Merely to ask that question is to step beyond the confines of this story. But we must hint at it. Nkrumah's task was much, *much* more than merely to drive out the British. He was calling his people from their Eden-like allegiances to their dead fathers and inspiring them to believe that they could master the ideas and techniques of the twentieth century. He was attempting to empty out the rich increment of the overburdened emotional consciousness of his tribal brothers and fasten that consciousness onto the brute, stark, workaday world in which it existed; and, at the same time, incite that consciousness to manipulate that world in the interests of his own deepest humanity.

On September 15, 1949, certain British officials actively entered the fight against Nkrumah by filing a series of libel suits, charging him with contempt of court. He was fined £300, a truly staggering blow for a newly created movement supported by penniless tribal people. But, within a matter of hours, the sum was raised voluntarily by the people of the streets. This act, more than anything else, convinced Nkrumah and his aides that their people were back of them, and they intensified their drive for self-government.

In October of 1949, the Coussey Committee's report was announced and Nkrumah called a monster mass meeting in Accra to study the constitutional proposals and decide to what extent they were acceptable. More than 80,000 people attended that meeting. The vast crowd objected to the three ex-officio members representing British vested interests being included in the cabinet; it protested against the suffrage age limit being set at twenty-five; it demanded a legislature composed of fully elected members instead of, as the report recommended, some being nominated and some being elected. The mass meeting advocated country-wide civil disobedience and non-co-operation if the British refused these demands.

During the first days of January of the following year, 1950, the Government invited the leaders of the Convention People's Party to a conference to discuss their proposals for constitutional change. The Government asked the nationalist leaders to postpone their campaign for civil disobedience until the Government had time to study what course to take. Nkrumah felt that such an attitude on the part of the Government indicated a ruse to stall for time; accordingly, twenty-four hours later, Nkrumah announced that "Positive Action" would begin.

On the morning of January 8, 1950, a colony-wide strike paralyzed the Gold Coast: not a train ran; buses and transportation trucks stood still; only water, electricity, health, and medical services were allowed to function. For twenty-one days, despite threats of dismissal of workers from jobs, martial law, warnings, curfews, and the full evocation of the emergency powers of the Governor, "Positive Action" and civil disobedience held sway in the Gold Coast. When it became evident that such action could continue indefinitely, the Governor again ordered the arrest of Nkrumah and the leaders of the Convention People's Party on charges of sedition. The trial lasted two months and ended with the conviction of all the leaders and their being sentenced to prison for terms varying from three months to four years.

During 1950, elections for town councils were held in the three largest cities of the Gold Coast: Accra, Kumasi, and Cape Coast. Though in prison, the leaders of the condemned party swept the polls, gaining decisive majorities wherever they had candidates running. When general elections were announced, the imprisoned leaders organized and conducted their campaigns from their prison cells! How was that possible? It was easy in the kind of tribal brotherhood that Nkrumah had established in his organization. The black jailers assigned by the Governor to guard the prisoners became the prisoners' messengers! They could not refuse to serve; first, they hotly wanted to see their land free of alien domination; second, they were bound by tribal loyalties to help their own brothers. Hence, the Convention People's Party was able to put up candidates in all of the country's constituencies. And from the leaders' prison cells political orders scribbled on toilet paper were smuggled out to the public by the men assigned to guard the prisoners! THESE MEN WERE ALREADY FREE! BUT THEY HAD TO PROVE IT WITH SACRIFICES! Were they willing to make those sacrifices? They were.

It was in prison that the greeting of "Freedom" was conceived and the salute of the elbow-resting-on-the-hip-and-the-right-palm-fronting-outward was invented. Nkrumah himself, while in his cell, wrote the party's song that would eventually be sung by the newly freed nation.

On February 8, 1951, the Convention People's Party swept the nation, winning thirty-five out of the thirty-eight seats. The people of the Gold Coast had elected as heads of the new government men who were in prison cells and the British had a new headache on their hands.

A few days later Nkrumah and his aides were told to dress in civilian clothes, an order that aroused their suspicions, for they thought that the British did not want the populace to see their newly elected leaders being transferred to another prison. But, no. It was freedom, an act of "grace," as the British quaintly called it for public consumption. But, privately, when speaking to the nationalist leaders themselves, the Governor admitted: "You chaps out-organized us." That was all. There was no mention of virtue; no talk of metaphysics; he didn't charge the African leaders with having progressed too fast. In short, his attitude said: "Well, you proved you were men. All right, you have the government." It was as simple as that.

Though Nkrumah had branded the constitution as being "bogus and fraudulent," he decided that his party would take a leading role in the new government for the following reasons: "We are going into the Government to show the world that the African can rule himself. We want the chance to fight for the political, social, and economic improvement of the country from both within and without the government."

This is a happy note upon which to end this story, but if I terminated my remarks here, I'd not be true to you or to the efforts of the Gold Coast Africans. Soon after he had taken over the government, Nkrumah had trouble. Some sections of the once-powerful tribes of the Ashanti and a few elements among the backward natives of the Northern Territories, incited by disgruntled political leaders, threatened secession. Self-government and freedom were proving to be a hard and lonely road, a cold and anguishing life. They suddenly longed for the father-image of the white man, for their warm and ancient days. They rebelled, rioted, shouted slogans against the new government, and called for a federal constitution that would enable them to follow their ancient folkways. Nkrumah stood firm against these new onslaughts from his own people and insisted that they march ahead. After much agitation, elections were held, in 1956, on the issue of whether there should be a strong central government or a loose federation of small local states, each with its own autonomous folkways. The idea of a strong central government, oriented towards an industrial future, won, as it should have.

In March 1957, the Gold Coast, under the leadership of Nkrumah, assumed independent status with full responsibility for its present and future, and its name was changed to Ghana.

Let us pause here and glance back over this story. In one sense, it is a glorious tale of men succeeding against almost impossible odds. But in another sense it is a stupid and tragic story. WHAT WAS THE FIGHT IN THE GOLD COAST ALL ABOUT? The issue was something so simple and human that one is almost ashamed to mention it. One set of men, black in color, had to organize and pledge their lives and make grievous sacrifices in order to prove to another set of men, white in color, that they were human beings! What a perversion of the energies of human life! What a reduction of human dignity comes about when men must consecrate their end-all and their be-all merely to prove that they are human beings. Suppose all of that energy had been put to embellishing the life of that country? What life-furthering gains there could have been!

But the black men involved had no choice. To maintain their position of psychological luxury stemming from the cheap and vulgar superiority of race domination, the white British had branded the black Gold Coasters as inferior, and those black men had no choice but to accept that challenge before they could do anything else. This useless struggle of having to prove one's humanity, which is a kind of *supra* racism, is the blight that the Western white man has cast upon the colored masses of Asia and Africa.

But the struggle in the Gold Coast is not over. The European has been driven from power there, but can the African drive out of himself that religious weakness that enabled the European to enter his land so easily and remain there as master for centuries? Can the African get *Africanism* out of Africa? Can the African overcome his ancestor-worshiping attitudes and learn to doubt the evidence of his senses as Descartes taught the Europeans to do, and master the techniques of science and develop a spirit of objectivity?

I can say one thing with certainty: The Gold Coast African now knows what he needs most to do. He needs to trade with the world; he needs the learning of the world; he needs the industrial disciplines and scientific facts of the world. What he does not need is bossing, white masters, racial snobbery, and the white man's concept of what is "good" for him.

Let us pause here and ask some pertinent questions. If the people of the Gold Coast had accepted the advice of the British, could they have won their independence so quickly and effectively? The answer is a categoric no. Only Africans, giving African solutions to African problems, could have accomplished that miracle. What politicians or academic spokesmen of the Western world would have dared, even merely imaginatively, to envisage the confounding unity of so many disparities which Nkrumah forged into so masterful a whole? None. What Nkrumah did had not only been declared impossible, unsound; but it was immoral. Why? For the simple reason that it had never been done before.

Do you know that even scientists and academic people, too, have their mysticism, their superstition? According to their feelings, that which has never happened before must somehow be wrong; and especially is this the attitude they hold in the sphere of human relations. It is for this reason that, no matter what happens in the Gold Coast, the Africans there are stoutly determined to decide for themselves what is good or bad for them.

The new government plans to construct a gigantic hydro-electric project by damming up rivers and creating one of the world's largest inland lakes. The idea is to use the electric power to manufacture aluminum out of bauxite, of which there is enough to last two hundred years. What do they plan to do with the aluminum? They want to swap it for atomic piles! In short, the Gold Coast is planning to launch itself directly into the twentieth century, with its present tribal structure and all. Well, why not? Why should the people of the Gold Coast repeat the slow, costly, and stupid industrial growth of the Western world?

Of course, the academic people have declared that that is wrong. Why? Well, it has just never happened before, so it's wrong. I say that, as yet, the world does not know what is "right" or "wrong" in such matters. I say that Nkrumah is right to plunge ahead and experiment. If such experiments are honestly and intelligently conducted, one cannot really lose. Even if failure attends the enterprise, one will have learned something, and a few new facts about man's life on earth will have been added to our stock of human knowledge.

Whenever and wherever I've explained this problem, I've been deluged with questions from Western whites:

"How can we help the Africans? Can we go to Africa and work with them? Will the Africans accept us?"

Yes, you can work with and help the Africans, and they will accept you if you can work with them in the spirit of civil *servants* rather than civil *masters*.

But, in my opinion, the greatest aid that any white Westerner can give Africa is by becoming a missionary right in the heart of the Western world, explaining to his own people what they have done to Africa. To those of you who fervently long to go to Africa, I say, beware. Africa is a most dangerous psychological trap. The millions of naked blacks living there in poetic dreams beckon seductively to the white misfits, the white failures, the white psychological cripples of the Western world. If you can't adjust to the exacting conditions of life in New York, or London, or Paris, or Berlin, then go to Africa and play God to simple-minded men. Only a mentally stunted and botched white man would want to obtain that kind of cheap salvation. Every white man desiring to go to Africa ought to be subjected to a most rigorous psychoanalytic examination to determine whether he is really emotionally fit to do so. Until today, the most tenacious enemies of Africa have been emotionally deformed white men hanging like millstones about Africa's neck.

What Africans need, above all, is an understanding on the part of others of what has happened to them. They know now, in part, what has happened to them, but the white men who caused that catastrophe do not know it. More than techniques, which they need, more than Point Fours, which they need, more than loans and gifts, which they need and can use, Africans need a simple acknowledgment from the white West of what it did. And that terribly human gesture, to be frank—men being what they are—is about the last thing that the white West can give Africa. It's too human a thing to ask, and, even if the West could give it, it would help the West even more than it would help Africa. For one thing, it would mean that the white man would not again, acting upon a ridiculous delusion, attempt to conquer lands in the name of a superior god or race. And that assurance would leave the newly freed African in psychological peace for a while to find himself and rebuild his shattered existence.

Can this happen? Is the West free enough of its own fears to let these people know that they will not be resubjugated? That is the question.

The Secret Circle that launched this revolution looked at their people through Western eyes, or they could not have pitted their puny strength against the might of Britain and the traditions of their people. Being Western, they were rightfully impatient; they wished to move ahead fast and create that world that would make them feel at home; they wanted to know that the earth upon which they lived and the men about them were not hostile. Western white men can understand these nationalist Africans if racial jealousy can be drained out of their hearts and if moral imperialism can be purged from their sensibilities.

If my words have any weight with you, I say, when you look at these black nationalists, you are looking at yourselves in another guise. But need that fact upset you? Need it incite you to anger? In order to contemplate one's life in an alien guise, one must have a clean heart, or else one is prone to project out upon that alien life one's own dirt, one's own spite, one's own self-hate, one's own inhibited impulses. Too long has Africa been made into a psychological garbage heap where white men dumped that part of themselves that they did not like. A free Africa will not only mean a chance of life for millions of people who have been victimized for centuries, but it will be a sign, too, that at long last the white man has grown up and has no longer any need to crucify others in order to feel normal. In sum, a free Africa presupposes a free mankind.

But, let me repeat one word of warning: The white man injected race feeling in Africa. And the easiest, the cheapest, the most vulgar, and the least worthy road that the African can travel is to become a racist like the white man, which would mean that the African has learned his lesson too bitterly and too well. To steer clear of the foul road of racism is not left to the decision of the African; too much pressure upon him can take him down that road, and, if he goes, and if the Asians follow him, then the vile logic of racism, which the white man helped to sow in this world, will grow and bear its blighted fruit.

We have it within our will and power to see that that does not happen.

Would it not be better to have continents of Asians and Africans wedded to practical goals than have them arming and mobilizing to make the world accept them as men? We make the world in which we live. So far we've made it a racist world. But surely such a world is not worthy of man as we dream of him and want him to be.